CONTENTS

NEW DIRECTIONS FOR INSTITUTIONAL RESEARCH

J. Fredericks Volkwein, *Penn State University*
EDITOR-IN-CHIEF

Larry H. Litten, *Dartmouth College*
ASSOCIATE EDITOR

What Is Institutional Research All About? A Critical and Comprehensive Assessment of the Profession

J. Fredericks Volkwein
Penn State University

EDITOR

Number 104, Winter 1999

JOSSEY-BASS PUBLISHERS
San Francisco

WHAT IS INSTITUTIONAL RESEARCH ALL ABOUT? A CRITICAL
AND COMPREHENSIVE ASSESSMENT OF THE PROFESSION
J. Fredericks Volkwein (ed.)
New Directions for Institutional Research, no. 104
Volume XXVI, Number 4
J. Fredericks Volkwein, Editor-in-Chief

New Directions for Institutional Research is indexed in *College Student
Personnel Abstracts, Contents Pages in Education,* and *Current Index to Jour-
nals in Education* (ERIC).

Microfilm copies of issues and chapters are available in 16mm and 35mm,
as well as microfiche in 105mm, through University Microfilms Inc., 300
North Zeeb Road, Ann Arbor, Michigan 48106-1346.

ISSN 0271-0579   ISBN 0-7879-1406-1

NEW DIRECTIONS FOR INSTITUTIONAL RESEARCH is part of The Jossey-Bass
Higher and Adult Education Series and is published quarterly by Jossey-
Bass Inc., Publishers, 350 Sansome Street, San Francisco, California
94104-1342 (publication number USPS 098-830). Periodicals postage
paid at San Francisco, California, and at additional mailing offices. POST-
MASTER: Send address changes to New Directions for Institutional
Research, Jossey-Bass Inc., Publishers, 350 Sansome Street, San Francisco,
California 94104-1342.

SUBSCRIPTIONS cost $56.00 for individuals and $99.00 for institutions,
agencies, and libraries.

EDITORIAL CORRESPONDENCE should be sent to J. Fredericks Volkwein,
Center for the Study of Higher Education, Penn State University, 403
South Allen Street, Suite 104, University Park, PA 16801-5252.

Photograph of the library by Michael Graves at San Juan Capistrano by
Chad Slattery © 1984. All rights reserved.

www.josseybass.com

Printed in the United States of America on acid-free recycled paper con-
taining 100 percent recovered waste paper, of which at least 20 percent is
postconsumer waste.

EDITOR'S NOTES

New Directions for Institutional Research was first published in 1974, under the leadership of Sidney Suslow and Paul Jedamus. Thus 1999 is the silver anniversary year for the *New Directions for Institutional Research* (NDIR) series.

To commemorate that twenty-fifth anniversary, this concluding volume of 1999 provides an overview of the field of institutional research and a status report on the profession. The editors have assembled a collection of chapters that collectively describe and analyze, blending both the theoretical and the practical sides of our endeavors. Who are we, and where are we going? What is institutional research all about? What tools does it use? How is it practiced in various settings? What are the trends in the field?

Many chapters commissioned for this volume offer useful conceptual frameworks for describing our profession. Others summarize the results of the various national and regional studies that have examined institutional researchers and institutional research (IR) offices and their functions. Several offer us a forecast of what lies ahead for institutional researchers.

As suggested in Chapter One, anniversaries are occasions for looking both forward and backward. The *NDIR* Series has been blessed with good leadership and solid support, both from the publishing team at Jossey-Bass in San Francisco and from the Association for Institutional Research (AIR) office in Tallahassee. Moreover the AIR Publications Committee has been a steady partner over the years, giving wise advice and guidance to the editors-in-chief. As you can see from the following list, the Volkwein-Litten team has a rich editorial heritage to build on.

Editors in Chief	*Associate Editors*
Sidney Suslow and	Patrick T. Terenzini, 1983–1984
Paul Jedamus, 1973–1977	Marvin W. Peterson, 1985–1989
Paul Jedamus, 1977–1978	Ellen E. Chaffee, 1990–1993
Marvin W. Peterson, 1978–1984	J. Fredericks Volkwein, 1994–1995
Patrick T. Terenzini, 1985–1995	Larry L. Litten, 1996–
J. Fredericks Volkwein, 1995–	

Sidney Suslow was an early advocate for this publication, and he found a strong ally in Paul Jedamus. The series received a solid beginning under their leadership. The first four *NDIR* volumes commissioned by Suslow and Jedamus are devoted to topics that are as relevant today as they were then: accountability, faculty workload, affirmative action, and nontraditional study. The next five years in the 1970s produced volumes on such important topics as student progress, resource allocation, planning, computing, interinstitutional arrangements, and academic productivity.

Marvin Peterson raised the series to a high level during his dozen years of active involvement as associate editor and editor. He commissioned volumes that addressed program evaluation, campus autonomy, professional development, marketing, retrenchment, assessment, attrition, and financial aid, among others. The series then benefited from the impressive thirteen-year leadership of Patrick Terenzini. The readership grew to its highest levels during the late 1980s, and volumes addressed topics ranging from information systems to legal issues, from research methods to policy analysis, from diversity to student tracking.

Of course, none of this would be possible without the host of willing and productive editors and authors who contribute their scholarship so unselfishly. The vitality and quality of each NDIR volume depends upon the thoughtful work of many. The list of editors and authors who have contributed to the 104 volumes of this series reads like a "Who's Who" in higher education and provides a profile of scholarly activity in the profession.

Table 1 summarizes the NDIR topics and volume editors since 1974. The first column lists institutional research topics grouped according to the AIR Forum Tracks, and the second column lists the volume numbers and editors in each group. Some volumes span multiple topics and therefore appear in more than one place in the table.

This exercise groups the 104 volumes into clusters as small as 6 in the theory and practice track, and as large as 26 in the track for effectiveness and assessment.

Track 1 includes the core area of enrollment management, addressed by eight separate volumes, five of them in the 1990s (those numbered 65 and above). This category includes Ernest Pascarella's volume (no. 36), *Studying Student Attrition,* which is one of the three most popular NDIR volumes in terms of total sales.

Track 2, institutional effectiveness, assessment, accountability, and improvement, has received greatest NDIR attention, with twenty-six volumes, spread across the early, middle, and late years of the series. This important area of NDIR activity includes the all-time best-seller *Assessing Educational Outcomes,* edited by Peter Ewell (no. 47).

The series has published eight volumes devoted to academic program and faculty issues (Track 3), but only three of these in the 1990s (edited by Braxton, Frost, and Wergin). This may be an area deserving more attention.

The fourth track addresses resource management topics. Here we find twenty-one volumes, with the majority of them appearing in the first ten years of the series and addressing issues related to resource allocation and reallocation.

Track 5 contains twenty-three policy, planning, and governance volumes, ranging from the earlier concentration on planning to the more recent attention given to organizational culture and climate. The Morrison, Refro, and Boucher volume (no. 39) on futures research is one of the three most popular sellers for NDIR.

Table 1. Classification of NDIR Volumes: 1974–1999

AIR Tracks and Topics	NDIR Volume Numbers and Editors
TRACK 1:	
Enrollment Management and Related Topics	70 Hossler
Enrollment forecasting	93 Layzell
Retention, attrition, persistence, and student tracking	36 Pascarella
	87 Ewell
Graduate student retention and time to degree	80 Baird
Financial aid	25 Henry
	62 Fenske
	95 Voorhees
TRACK 2:	
Institutional Effectiveness, Assessment,	29 Miller
Accountability, and Improvement	32 Lindquist
Accountability, performance measures, quality	1 Bowen
assurance	16 Folger
	82 Borden and Banta
	99 Gaither
	97 Burke and Serban
Academic program reviews and evaluating	27 Craven
administrative services	86 Barak and Mets
	41 Scott
	56 Wergin and Braskamp
Guidebooks, rankings, and ratings	88 Walleri and Moss
Alumni studies, fund raising, and market research	21 Lucas
	54 Lay and Endo
	60 Melchiori
	101 Pettit and Litten
Outcomes assessment	47 Ewell
	59 Banta
Student characteristics and climate	98 Bauer
Nontraditional study	4 Baskin
Graduate education and research	50 Cresswell
	80 Baird
	90 Braxton
	92 Haworth
Quality management (TQM and CQI)	71 Sherr and Teeter
	78 Teeter and Lozier
TRACK 3:	
Academic Program and Faculty Issues	57 Stark and Mets
	90 Braxton
Academic management	10 Smart and Montgomery
	100 Frost
Faculty workload and productivity	2 Doi
	83 Wergin

(*continued*)

Table 1. Classification of NDIR Volumes: 1974–1999 (*continued*)

AIR Tracks and Topics	NDIR Volume Numbers and Editors
Faculty evaluation and development	20 Kirschling
	50 Cresswell
Teaching and faculty	57 Stark and Mets
	90 Braxton
TRACK 4:	
Resource Management	8 Wallhaus
	11 Dressel and Simon
	13 Hopkins and Schroeder
Pricing and cost analysis	17 Gonyea
	42 Litten
	75 Hollins
Human resource management	7 Heist and Warren
Managing faculty resources	18 Leslie
	40 Baldwin and Blackburn
	63 Lozier and Dooris
Managing change, decline, restructuring	6 Cartter
	24 Cooke
	30 Hample
	33 Hipps
	79 Simpson
	94 Norris
	100 Frost
Endowment and fundraising	51 Dunn
	43 Leslie
Forecasting revenues	93 Layzell
Facilities and space analysis	61 Kaiser
TRACK 5:	
Policy, Planning, and Governance	26 Dressel
Planning and strategic planning	13 Hopkins and Schroeder
	19 Fenske
	28 Heydinger
	33 Hipps
	37 Uhl
	52 Callan
	67 Schmidtlein and Milton
Environmental analysis and forecasting	39 Morrison, Refro, and Boucher
	52 Callan
Policy analysis	76 Gill and Saunders
Leadership, trustees, boards	5 Berdahl
Culture, climate, diversity, teamwork	3 Sells
	65 Nettles
	68 Tierney
	81 Smith, Wolf, and Levitan

AIR Tracks and Topics	NDIR Volume Numbers and Editors
Culture, climate, diversity, teamwork *(contd.)*	98 Bauer
	100 Frost
Campus and government relations and regulations	45 Hodgkinson
Athletics	74 Mallette and Howard
Legal issues	14 Taylor
	48 Rosenthal and Yancey
	96 Jones
TRACK 6: **Theory, Practice, and Ethics of Institutional Research**	38 Firnberg and Lasher
	46 Peterson and Corcoran
	66 Presley
	104 Volkwein
Developing the new or small IR office	66 Presley
Ethics in IR	73 Schiltz
Career development	23 Cope
TRACK 7: **Technology, Tools, Skills**	102 Katz and Rudy
	103 Sanders
Development and evaluation of information and computing technology	9 Mason
	22 Staman
	31 Poulton
	44 Tetlow
	55 Stamen
	85 Sanford
	102 Katz and Rudy
	103 Sanders
Student information and tracking systems	35 Sheehan
	87 Ewell
MIS and decision support systems	15 Adams
	31 Poulton
	44 Tetlow
	49 Rohrbaugh and McCartt
	64 Ewell
	77 Glover and Krotseng
	84 Kinnick
Data management and exchange	55 Stamen
	69 Lenth
	89 Trainer
Interinstitutional peer comparison	12 Peterson
	53 Brinkman
Statistics and research methods	58 Yancey
Qualitative research methods	34 Kuhns and Martorana
	72 Fetterman
Factbook development	91 Jones

The sixth cluster contains the seven volumes, such as this one, where we study ourselves. *NDIR* has felt the need to do this only about twice each decade.

The Track 7 group includes twenty-eight volumes that focus on technology and research tools. Over the years, *NDIR* editors have experienced a steady demand for volumes that collect the latest and best information about needed skills and available tools for the efficient and effective practice of institutional research.

This twenty-five-year history sets the context for the current volume. First, J. Fredericks Volkwein's chapter identifies the "four faces" of institutional research: describing the institution, analyzing alternatives, presenting the best case, and supplying impartial evidence. Volkwein gives us an overview of the issues and tensions that face institutional researchers as they carry out their work, and he reviews five current policy issues that collide on the campus, indicating how they add to the complexities of practicing institutional research. The chapter concludes with the four-part typology of IR purposes and roles that reflects the issues, tensions, and dualistic nature of the field.

The second chapter is a reprint of Patrick T. Terenzini's classic text on the three tiers of organizational intelligence—technical/analytical intelligence, issues intelligence, and contextual intelligence. Most important to institutional research practitioners, Terenzini's chapter specifically addresses the ways in which each domain of institutional research knowledge and skills may best be acquired.

In their chapter, William E. Knight, Michael E. Moore, and Corby A. Coperthwaite examine effectiveness in institutional research with a survey instrument based on Terenzini's three levels of organizational intelligence. Most IR respondents report that they possess technical/analytical intelligence and issues intelligence, but contextual intelligence was less evident. The survey items produced five factors rather than three, and the strongest was a global factor reflecting general institutional research knowledge and skills. Because the study explains only 17 percent of the variance in the self-reported measure of effectiveness, the authors conclude that additional studies like this one are needed.

Next, Sarah B. Lindquist synthesizes much of the available information on institutional researchers and the institutions that employ them. Her research for this chapter uncovered five national surveys of the AIR membership over the last two decades; these surveys included items that can be used to develop a profile of the personal and organizational characteristics of individuals in our profession. She reviews an array of data from the national AIR office, from membership surveys since 1981, and from selected annual forum evaluations to address the questions: Who are we? Where do we work? and What do we do? She finds surprising stability in the descriptive characteristics of IR members and their institutions over the past two decades, especially when one considers the growth in the field. She presents a statistical profile of the "average" institutional researcher.

In the fifth chapter, John A. Muffo examines the half dozen or so regional studies of institutional research offices in North America, studies conducted by the Northeast Association for Institutional Research and the Southern Association for Institutional Research, among others. He notes especially their focus on IR size, organizational location, professional preparation, and primary tasks. Together, the Lindquist and Muffo chapters suggest similar patterns in the findings of the studies they examined: IR office size is dependent on institution size; smaller IR offices are more likely to report to the institution president and larger IR offices are more likely to report to a vice president; larger offices tend to have more highly trained and experienced staff carrying out a more complex array of analytical tasks; and all IR offices are heavily engaged in standardized reporting externally and internally and in enrollment management studies. Muffo believes that these profiles will be influenced in the years ahead by emerging trends in the four areas of technology, demographics, pedagogy, and national and state policy.

Frank A. Schmidtlein, in the sixth chapter, discusses the organizational assumptions that often mislead institutional researchers and their clients. He reviews emerging organizational theory that suggests limitations to the use of data and analysis in decision making. Particular emphasis is placed on the role of *nonquantitative intelligence* in decision making and its relationship to the data and analysis provided by institutional researchers. Opportunities to apply data analysis in decision making seem to be on the rise along with the importance of the role of such analysis, and Schmidtlein suggests a framework through which institutional researchers can view the issues that confront their institutions in order to better assist in decision-making efforts.

Next, Mark Bagshaw offers tips for coping with the learning-inhibited institution. Individual and organizational learning theory suggests that several critical features of higher education institutions may inhibit learning. Institutional research can play a major role in improving an institution's ability to learn; however, Bagshaw describes the institutionalization, concerns over legitimacy, dispersion of authority, and other factors that hinder institutional learning and acceptance of institutional research. In addition to identifying disabling characteristics, he proposes practical solutions institutional researchers can use to combat an institution's inhibitions about learning. Overall, Bagshaw argues for a proactive stance with regard to IR interactions in institutions.

To conclude this volume, Marvin W. Peterson revisits his earlier writings and giving us a descriptive and analytical update of the field and where he thinks we are headed. His chapter includes a review of the history of institutional research and an analysis of the forces at work in postsecondary education; the challenges of the twenty-first century, including the emerging knowledge industry; and the new roles for IR that he believes will evolve. This final chapter, in particular, notes the demand for knowledge industry analysts and emphasizes the critical need for institutional researchers to fulfill this vital role.

As with all of our volumes, we hope that this one provides useful information that enhances the practice of the profession.

J. Fredericks Volkwein
Editor
Steven LaNasa

J. FREDERICKS VOLKWEIN is director, professor, and senior scientist at the Center for the Study of Higher Education, Penn State University.

STEVEN LANASA, a doctoral student at Penn State University, assisted with the overall preparation of this volume.

1

*This chapter describes the purposes and roles of
institutional researchers–to describe the institution,
to analyze alternatives, to present the best case, and to
supply impartial evidence—and summarizes the conflicts
researchers face as they attempt to fulfill them.*

The Four Faces
of Institutional Research

J. Fredericks Volkwein

The ancient Roman god Janus was the god of doors and gateways. Like the two sides of a door, Janus has two faces—one looking outward and one looking inward. While Janus encourages us to consider both the external and the internal aspects of our endeavors, Janusian thinking also reminds us that when we pass through a door we are simultaneously entering and leaving. Thus one action viewed in opposite ways recognizes the dual nature of almost everything we do. Commencement is both an ending and a beginning. For every action there is a reaction.

All individuals in colleges and universities experience such dualities. This chapter gives some prominent examples and suggests some conflicting roles that institutional researchers confront.

Dualities in Colleges and Universities

There are three kinds of opposing pressures in postsecondary institutions that are particularly relevant to institutional researchers: internal demands may contrast with external demands, the academic culture differs from the administrative culture, and the institutional needs may vary from professional needs.

Duality 1: The Internal Versus the External. Presidents and vice presidents direct much time and energy toward internal management. But they also interact with key people in the external environment and indeed attempt to shape that environment in order to maximize institutional resources. When interacting with key external stakeholders (like trustees and legislators), presidents must appear to be in strong control of the educational

NEW DIRECTIONS FOR INSTITUTIONAL RESEARCH, no. 104, Winter 1999 © Jossey-Bass Publishers organization and able to deliver on promised programs and initiatives. Back at home, however, presidents and provosts face major internal impediments to change: consensus governance, faculty control over the major goal activities, an organizational culture that supports change by adding resources rather than by reallocating resources, and a curriculum structure that makes false assumptions about learner homogeneity. University presidents should be forceful leaders, but they should never interfere with faculty democracy. Decisions should be made swiftly, but everyone should be consulted ahead of time. Clark Kerr complained that his faculty at the University of California at Berkeley expected him to be a mouse at home but a lion abroad.

Duality 2: Academic Versus Administrative Cultures. Universities are fascinating organizations because they house at least two strong cultures within the same organizational structure. One is the administrative culture, the bureaucracy, where authority and responsibility are based largely on one's position or rank. Among the administrative offices that compose the bureaucracy, communication and decision making are largely hierarchical and based on division of labor and delegated responsibility. The other culture, of course, is the faculty's academic culture, the professional culture, where authority is based not so much on one's position as on one's knowledge or expertise. In the academic department, communication and decision making are more collegial.

Moreover, the organization's goal activities (teaching, research, service) are carried out by the academic culture, which places a high value on quality and effectiveness. The administrative bureaucracy supplies the support services; this culture is much more cost conscious and places a high value on efficiency. Thus faculty and administrators live in organizational cultures that are importantly different. Their varied approaches and values often produce organizational tensions for institutional researchers and others who must operate in both cultures.

Because institutional research (IR) operates in both of these contrasting cultures, it may be thought of as a halfway house. Our efforts and analytical work are administratively directed because our data inform managerial decision making—and we know who signs our paychecks. But some of our work (like faculty workload analysis and assessment) takes us into the academic culture. The IR office serves at times as a home for theory-driven social science research but more often as a practice-oriented detective agency. We are trained as researchers, and some of us hire graduate assistants or draw upon faculty expertise to help us with our research, in the same way that an academic department does. But unlike the academic department's work, our research sometimes is for the president's inner circle only.

Duality 3: Institutional Versus Professional Roles. Faculty in most universities experience tension between their institutional role (teaching) and their professional role (scholarship). For the most part, faculty are hired to teach particular subjects, but they are trained and rewarded, at least in universities, for their research and scholarship. Only occasionally do uni-

versity faculty receive formal training for the role they have been hired for—
teaching students. Moreover, the products of teaching are generally less visible than the products of research, so most faculty are given promotion and
tenure (and professional mobility) based largely on their research and scholarship.

Institutional researchers may face a similar role tension when they are
hired to produce accurate numbers and descriptive statistics about the campus (the institutional role) but are trained for and find fulfillment in the
challenges of research and analysis (the professional role).

These three dualities constantly rub against each other, and the tensions they produce are greatly exacerbated by the conflicts among five public policy concerns.

Collision of Five Policy Concerns

An array of public policy issues intersect on the campus and challenge all
of us in higher education. The first is a concern about the high cost of a college education—a concern expressed by parents, college students, and tax-
payers alike. Since 1970, tuition and fees on both public and private
campuses have risen on average at a rate that is *double* the increases in the
Consumer Price Index.

A second policy concern is the almost universal need for management
efficiency and increased productivity. Public concern about high cost mag-
nifies concern about low productivity. Virtually every sector of the nation's
economy has made substantial gains in productivity in the past thirty years;
yet in higher education, salaries and cost per student have been rising at
rates well above inflation. Colleges and universities use more resources in
relation to outputs than before, and economists call that declining productivity. Many trustees and state legislators have business backgrounds, and
for them, the idea of restructuring and becoming more productive is a familiar necessity. However, few faculty see it this way.

The third public concern focuses on universities' and colleges' effectiveness. Most customers are willing to pay more for higher quality and better service, but it is not clear that higher tuition prices translate into higher
quality. In fact there is ample evidence from employers and researchers alike
that many college graduates are not as well educated, nor as employable, as
they were in the past and as they need to be in the future. For example, the
National Adult Literacy Survey found that large numbers of two-year and
four-year college graduates are unable to use basic skills in everyday situations involving reading, writing, arithmetic computation, and elementary
problem solving. The Wingspread Group on Higher Education (1993) con-
cluded that a bachelor's degree seems to be a credential without content.

A fourth policy issue is access. The national value system in the United
States demands that access to higher education should be provided to all.
Most families see higher education as the vehicle for upward mobility and

a ticket to the "good life" for their children. Certainly in public higher education, student access is a significant if not controlling mission, but public and private institutions alike have expanded their commitments to educational opportunity and have used this commitment to justify additional funding.

The fifth policy issue is accountability. Both public and private institutions have stakeholders who do not necessarily agree that campus autonomy is a good thing. At the very least, they believe that campuses need to be held accountable for fulfilling their educational missions (Bowen, 1974). At the extreme, they believe that campuses need to be micro-managed in order to ensure efficient operation and the attainment of strategic goals. Such views are in plentiful supply, not only at the trustee and local level but also at the state and national levels.

When these five competing concerns about cost, productivity, access, effectiveness, and accountability all collide at the campus level, they create an array of campus tensions for planners, institutional researchers, and administrators at all levels.

Tension 1: Campus Autonomy, Public Accountability, and Government Regulation. There has been much public discussion about the virtues of deregulation and decentralized, customer-based management. The business literature is filled with the advantages of hierarchically *flat* organizations that can move quickly and adapt to changing circumstances in the market. Even government bureaucracies are being encouraged to *reinvent* themselves. Most elected officials now recognize the value of academic autonomy, or at least give lip service to the ideal of government deregulation in public higher education. The recent atmosphere in Washington, D.C., and most state capitals reflects a growing consensus that regulation and control can be both costly and unproductive.

Nevertheless, these impulses conflict with the philosophy of public accountability. The concept of accountability in a bureaucratic democracy justifies the government's attempts to enforce sound management practices (Yates, 1982). The government acts in the public interest in part because higher education is now viewed as a social and political right rather than a privilege (Kerr, 1963). Access to higher education, facilitated by public funding, should be provided to every child and adult who seeks it. Thus, postsecondary institutions, as agents of this national policy, become accountable to the general public interest (Mortimer, 1972). This perspective creates a climate that justifies intrusive state and federal policies. In some states, financial and personnel transactions at public colleges and universities receive redundant scrutiny by central system offices, legislative committees, and state executive staff (Volkwein, 1987). Most politicians, not wanting to appear unresponsive, are quick to jump on the latest media-hyped story of some campus incident or indiscretion, and use it as an excuse to pass yet another piece of legislation or reporting requirement. So there are now myriad state and federal regulations and reporting requirements related to affirmative action, Americans with disabilities, athletics, freedom of information, clean air, campus crime, financial accounting requirements, fuel use and contamination, occupational health and safety, purchasing practices, personnel benefits, payroll transactions, research involving human subjects, research involving warm-blooded animals, radiation safety, student financial aid, waste disposal, and student privacy rights, the list goes on. "Taken by itself, any single action may not be unbearably intrusive, but the combined impact of many actions can nearly suffocate an institution" (Carnegie Foundation, 1982, p. 65). To make matters worse, the public and our elected officials then act surprised, perhaps even dismayed, when discovering that two-thirds of the postsecondary education workforce are engaged in activities outside the classroom.

Tension 2: Access, Excellence, and Accountability. Simultaneous pressures for access, excellence, and accountability create an enrollment management dilemma: colleges and universities experience opposite enrollment pressures—they are asked to simultaneously admit more students (for financial health and access) and become more selective (to bolster academic standards and performance measures). Janus is alive and well.

On the one hand campuses need student enrollments (and the revenue that comes with them) in the current competitive enrollment-driven economy in which 90 percent of accredited institutions of higher education in North America admit over 90 percent of their applicants (Volkwein, 1995). Most, though not all, campuses have a self-interest in admitting and retaining a huge proportion of their applicants as a matter of economic survival.

On the other hand many applicants (though I hope not many at your campus) have poor records of prior achievement and are not good risks for acceptable academic performance and graduation. Moreover, faculty have concerns about academic standards—concerns that are usually reflected in pressures for selective admissions. And here is the rub: we would all like to ignore the old elitist resource and reputation model with its overemphasis on maximizing the inputs in order to guarantee the quality of the outputs. However, the truth is that a number of extremely important outcomes are highly predictable from the inputs. We can predict about one-third of the variance in student academic performance and two-thirds of the variance in persistence to graduation by knowing the high school rank in class and SAT scores of freshmen (Volkwein, 1995). Poor academic performance is the number one reason for student departure, and departure before degree completion is the number one reason for loan default (Volkwein, 1995). Maintaining selective admissions standards, therefore, is a viable enrollment management and loan default reduction strategy because it improves campus performance on three highly visible accountability measures—rates of new student persistence, rates of graduation, and rates of loan default.

The good news is that U.S. college students have more variety, choice, and access than at any time in history—and more than students anywhere else in the world. The bad news is that U.S. institutions face severe competition, not only for students but for faculty and other resources as well. They devote considerable campus resources to the processes of recruiting, financing, and retaining diverse populations of both faculty and students in the fiercely competitive environment. These competitive pressures, by the way, lower institutional productivity, because they prevent colleges and universities from investing more directly and heavily in their primary goal activities of teaching, research, and service. Instead, institutions hire more staff to help in necessary support areas like admissions, financial aid, government relations, fundraising, student advisement, and an array of faculty and student support services. Why? Because in an atmosphere of accountability, competition, and enrollment-driven budgets, they cannot afford to ignore either the *quantity* or the *quality* of inputs.

Even so, throughout higher education we now see much greater interest among institutions and their stakeholders in measuring *outcomes*— judging the results. Although most of us are more comfortable with this approach, it runs the danger of providing information too late in the process to render anything but a summative, or acceptable versus unacceptable, judgement. An overfocus on outcomes may not provide the information needed for internal development and educational enhancement.

Therefore there is now a renewed interest in process measures, rooted in the theory that good outcomes will not result from flawed educational processes. Measurement at critical process points enables institutions to determine which student experiences are having the greatest (and the least) impact and to make corrective interventions. Moreover, the research evidence indicates that many outcomes such as student growth and satisfaction are most heavily and favorably influenced by those campus experiences that produce student academic and social integration (Pascarella and Terenzini, 1991; Volkwein, 1992, 1993).

Thus we have for institutional researchers the ideal jobs bill:

The need to measure and improve inputs, because of the strong empirical connection between input measures and important outcomes like academic achievement, graduation rates, and loan default

The need to measure critical processes, both because of the role of these processes in student integration and growth and because such measurement facilitates corrective intervention

The need to measure a variety of outputs and outcomes, because results matter most

In short, we need to measure everything that moves.

Tension 3: Productivity Versus Outcomes. Parents believe and research suggests that the most effective educational experiences are usually found in academically oriented living and learning communities in which full-time students receive a good deal of faculty contact and many academic support services in the residential setting (Pascarella and Terenzini, 1991).

However, we also know that being educated within these highly effective living and learning communities is expensive when compared to being educated via the new information technologies. The dilemma is that parents and students desire the more personal learning experience that comes with traditional settings, but the public demand for access and productivity encourages legislators to give a high priority to distance learning and to encourage the use of technology to instruct larger numbers of students with fewer faculty.

The rub is that it's easier and cheaper to transmit information using computer assisted instruction than it is to teach students to think. The danger is that technology will provide greater access but diminish educational quality. The challenge is to use information technology in ways that assist individualized learning. This will probably not translate into a need for fewer faculty. And it may not even be cheaper! There is an emerging rule of thumb that in order to stay current, an institution should spend at least 5 percent of its annual budget on information technology.

Tension 4: Cost and Efficiency Versus Quality and Effectiveness. In 1995, the State University of New York (SUNY) trustees issued a document called *Rethinking SUNY*. This report, aimed at restructuring the SUNY system, lowering its cost, and increasing its productivity, struck many of us as overemphasizing indicators of cost and efficiency, and underemphasizing indicators of quality and effectiveness. It is easier for centralized authority to count the number of students in the classroom than to measure what they are learning. It is easier to count the square feet of campus space in use than to discover how well the space is being used.

Another interesting development occurred in that same year when the New York State Comptroller's Division of Management Audit issued its report on the state university's performance indicators. The audit assessed not only the extent to which SUNY's measures reflected progress toward the goals described in the planning document *SUNY 2000* but also the extent to which these measures were consistent with those contained in the Performance Reporting Model of the national Government Accounting Standards Board.

Surprisingly, this model developed by government accountants contains measures of performance that we might have designed ourselves, including ratings by students and alumni, retention and graduation rates, student performance on academic tests and professional examinations, rates of employment and graduate school attendance, and employer satisfaction. This is a refreshing change from legislative and trustee attention to things like class size, faculty contact hours, and student time to degree completion, measures that focus on means rather than ends—on the cost of the educational process rather than on the results.

At any rate, I believe that the planning environment for the foreseeable future means that higher education will be viewed with increasingly critical eyes. And these eyes will focus with equal acuity on the education offered by traditional campuses and by the newer technologies. Outcomes assessment and performance measures are in danger of becoming a relatively permanent part of the educational enterprise.

Tension 5: Assessing for Internal Improvement Versus External Accountability. The classic Janusian challenge for most of us is resolving the tension between the internal and the external uses of assessment and performance. In public and private institutions alike, all individuals face the need to improve themselves and to become better teachers, learners, scholars, and administrators. To accomplish this, they need to expose their weaknesses and identify what needs to be changed. However, such openness runs the danger of reducing an institution's market appeal and its resources, especially in an atmosphere of fierce competition and performance funding. As one writer puts it, "The spirit of assessment requires a diligent search for bad news, but accountability encourages the opposite" (Peters, 1994, p. 17).

Various regional accrediting associations (most prominently the Middle States, Southern [SACS], and North Central [NCA]) attempt to resolve this tension by requiring each campus to present evidence of student learning and growth as a key component in demonstrating the institution's effectiveness. To be accredited each institution is expected to gather and present evidence that it is accomplishing its educational goals. The new Middle States monograph, *Framework for Outcomes Assessment* (Commission on Higher Education, 1996), is extremely helpful in that it provides guidance to campuses in assessment areas such as basic skills, general education, personal growth, and the major field of study.

Simply put, the institutional goal should be the improvement of student learning and growth. Campuses need to carry out assessment and self-evaluation not for external accountability but for internal enhancement. Outcomes assessment does not judge undergraduate education but improves it. Faculty, especially, identify with this emphasis.

Now for some realism: in an atmosphere of resource scarcity, campuses that can measure their effectiveness will do better in the competition for external resources than will campuses that cannot. And academic departments that are able to provide presidents and provosts with evidence about the impacts they are having on their students will be more successful in the competition for campus resources than will academic units not able to provide such evidence (Volkwein, 1995).

Thus the action by Middle States, NCA, and SACS properly calls our attention to two principal uses of assessment improvement and accountability. These dual emphases, these twin purposes, seem to offer a constructive path. They provide the motivation and foundation for internal development and at the same time recognize the need to demonstrate effectiveness to stakeholders.

The Four Faces of Institutional Research

I have discussed a variety of campus dualities, tensions, and policy colli-sions—internal versus external, academic versus administrative, professional versus institutional, access versus excellence, efficiency versus effectiveness, and assessing for improvement versus assessing for accountability. These contradictory pressures produce a variety of challenges for institutional researchers and force us to play a medley of roles. In our campus endeav-ors, we pursue a number of different purposes, summarized by the frame-work in Figure 1.1, which identifies four IR types.

On the horizontal axis of the matrix, this typology distinguishes between those IR purposes and audiences that are more formative, internal, and improvement oriented and those that are more summative, external, and accountability oriented. The vertical axis characterizes organizational roles and cultures in two ways: first, administrative and institutional, and second, academic and professional. As discussed earlier, the administrative culture is more consistent with bureaucratic values like efficiency, and the academic culture is more consistent with professional values like effective-ness. Combining these categories produces a typology of four overlapping yet distinguishable types of IR purposes and roles. These are not pure types, but they reflect dominant tendencies and can be applied either to the IR office as a whole or to the separate individuals and functions within it.

IR as Information Authority. The internal and administrative pur-pose and support role calls upon institutional research to describe the insti-tution's shape and size, its students and staff, and its activities. Here the institutional researcher educates the campus community about itself in terms of data on admissions, enrollment, faculty, and degrees awarded. Gen-erating most of the information in a factbook falls into this category. In this role the institutional researcher compiles and packages descriptive statistics for campus audiences. Of the many challenging IR tasks, this one probably requires the least preparation in the form of education and experience. The

Figure 1.1. Four Purposes and Roles of Institutional Research

	PURPOSES AND AUDIENCES	
ORGANIZATIONAL ROLE AND CULTURE	Formative and Internal— for Improvement	Summative and External— for Accountability
Administrative and Institutional	To describe the institution— IR as information authority	To present the best case— IR as spin doctor
Academic and Professional	To analyze alternatives— IR as policy analyst	To supply impartial evidence of effectiveness— IR as scholar and researcher

role requirements correspond roughly to Terenzini's description of technical intelligence (see Chapter Two).

IR as Policy Analyst. The internal and professional purpose calls upon IR to study and analyze the institution and its policies. In this role the institutional researcher works with top management as an analyst or consultant, providing support for planning and budget allocation decisions, policy revision, administrative restructuring, or other needed change. Here the institutional researcher is the policy analyst who educates the management team. Many of us are especially likely to assume this role when we conduct studies for our colleagues in academic affairs, budgeting, and student services. Falling into this category are studies that give alternative enrollment scenarios and revenue projections based upon different assumptions about inputs and attrition. Comparative cost analysis, student opinion research, and studies of salary equity are other examples. This role requires relatively high levels of education and training, as well as both analytical and issues intelligence (also described in Chapter Two).

IR as Spin Doctor. Of the two external types of IR, the administrative style is visible when IR assembles descriptive statistics that reflect favorably upon the institution. Many of us are called upon to play this advocate role frequently, and we need to protect against carrying this style to an unethical extreme. Here the IR staff present the *best case* for the campus, describing the glass as half full rather than half empty. Some would put our admissions material for students and parents in this category, but we certainly perform this role when we assist campus fundraisers and government relations staff in presenting a positive image. Some experience on the job and knowledge of the institution is usually needed for success in this role.

IR as Scholar and Researcher. The professionally oriented and analytical version of the external accountability role is that of the impartial researcher and scholar who investigates and produces evidence so that institutional effectiveness, legal compliance, and goal attainment can be judged. Conducting outcomes studies and performance reports when the primary audience is external to the campus falls into this category. Support for the accreditation of self-study might be another example. This is a sophisticated role that requires advanced training and years of experience.

Some IR activities are difficult to classify because they overlap several categories. A factbook has both internal and external audiences. Compliance reporting has both descriptive and analytical aspects. When we score and report student ratings, we act as the information authority, but we become the research analyst when we carry out studies based on student ratings data. Faculty workload and instructional analysis may appear in any of the four quadrants, depending on the audience and the complexity of the task.

Nevertheless, most of what we do forces us to play one or another of these roles, and sometimes two or more simultaneously. Although the boundaries around these four faces of institutional research may blur from time to time and the transition from one to the other may be as rapid as a telephone call, I'm convinced that my institution needs IR to play all four roles effectively. I suspect that yours does too.

J. Fredericks Volkwein is professor, senior scientist, and director of the Center for the Study of Higher Education at Penn State University.

2

Categorizing organizational intelligence into three tiers—technical/analytical intelligence, issues intelligence, and contextual intelligence—helps us to understand that our many roles and tasks mean we need varieties of knowledge and skills and that we must acquire them in different ways.

On the Nature of Institutional Research and the Knowledge and Skills It Requires

Patrick T. Terenzini

During the 1978 Association for Institutional Research (AIR) Forum in Houston, a hotel guest who was not part of the conference stepped into an elevator crowded with AIR members, including at least two past presidents. The guest looked at the organizational name tags and asked: "What's 'institutional research'?" The question was followed first by silence, then by nervous laughter. A dozen or so floors later, the doors opened to let the guest out, and there still had been no serious answer to the question.

One might reasonably argue that a dozen or so floors really does not afford sufficient time to answer the question seriously. The history of the question, of course, spans nearly a third of a century! One view, articulated by Nevitt Sanford (1962), saw institutional research (although he didn't use that label) as a series of long-term, theoretically based studies of institutional functioning and educational outcomes. John Dale Russell conceived of institutional researchers as having "'specific responsibility for carrying on studies needed for the making of important decisions about policy and procedure'; and . . . work[ing] toward the primary goal of finding out how 'to save money that can be used to better advantage'" (Dyer, 1966, pp. 453–454). For his part, Dyer predicted that if institutional research was to have any meaningful and enduring impact on institutional quality, "it

This chapter reprints a paper presented at the annual meeting of the Association for Institutional Research, San Francisco, May 1991. A revised version was subsequently published in *Research in Higher Education, 34* (1), 1993, pp. 1–10.

must somehow integrate *both* of these points of view in a common attack on institutional problems" (p. 454).

Others conceive of institutional research differently. Dressel (1971) asserts that "the basic purpose of institutional research is to probe deeply into the workings of an institution for evidence of weaknesses or flaws which interfere with the attainment of its purposes or which utilize an undue amount of resources in so doing" (p. 23). A decade later, Dressel (1981) wrote that "institutional research has to do with what decision makers need to know about an institution, its educational objectives, goals and purposes, environmental factors, processes, and structures to more wisely use its resources, more successfully attain its objectives and goals, and to demonstrate integrity and accountability in so doing" (p. 237). Saupe (1981, 1990) defines institutional research as "research conducted within an institution of higher education in order to provide information which supports institutional planning, policy formulation, and decision making" (p. 1). Saupe, like Fincher (1977), differentiates institutional research from research on higher education in that the latter focuses on the advancement of theory and knowledge of higher education generally, while the former is concerned with knowledge about a specific institution or system of institutions, and the generalizability of findings to other settings is not a primary concern. To the higher education researcher, knowledge of some aspect of a specific institution holds interest only to the extent that it is (or might be) generalizable to some larger set of individuals or institutions. To the institutional researcher, such knowledge is *inherently* interesting. Indeed, it is the raison d'être for institutional research.

Various chapters in Jedamus, Peterson, and Associates (1980) and Fincher (1985) offer other useful, if varying, definitions or descriptions of institutional research. Fincher, for example, explores the question of whether institutional research is a science, an art, or a little of both. McKinney and Hindera (1991) suggest some of the commonalities institutional research shares with science, but also point out where and how the two enterprises differ. Peterson (1985) traces the evolution of institutional research and AIR since their emergence in the early 1960s and concludes that both the definitions and activities of institutional research are to some extent dynamic over time.

Thus the definitional problem persists, as these authors and several recent [AIR] Forum sessions demonstrate. Moreover, the nature of institutional research and the role it plays on most campuses, as Peterson (1985) notes, continues to evolve as a consequence of state and federal policy decisions, the changing student clientele, advances in computing and telecommunications, the shifting budgetary climate, the growing internationalization of higher education, the increasing complexity and sophistication of decision making, and the growing number and volume of calls for increased institutional effectiveness.

This paper offers a conception of institutional research that grows out of existing definitions but is broad enough to accommodate the many changes taking place in the functions institutional researchers are asked to perform and the tools they use. The underlying view of institutional research taken here comes from Wilensky (1969) and Fincher (1978), who view institutional research as "organizational intelligence," as "a professional, technical specialty with strong resources and capabilities for policy-related research in institutions of higher education" (Fincher, 1985, p. 34). Here, however, the metaphor of organizational intelligence is construed somewhat more broadly to refer to the data gathered about an institution, to their analysis and transformation into information, and to the insight and informed sense of the organization that a competent institutional researcher brings to the interpretation of that information. This conception of institutional research implies three forms of personal competence and institutional understanding that are required. The paper also discusses the means by which such forms of intelligence might be acquired.

Forms of Organizational Intelligence

Three different but equally important and interdependent kinds of organizational intelligence are identifiable: *technical/analytical intelligence, issues intelligence,* and *contextual intelligence.* The ability to apply one's intelligence in a higher tier implies possession of the intelligence characteristic of lower tiers. For example, the capacity to function well in the issues tier implies possession of the appropriate technical/analytical intelligence.

Tier 1: Technical/Analytical Intelligence. This category of intelligence is of two kinds: factual knowledge or information, and analytical and methodological skills and competencies. The factual knowledge characteristic of technical/analytical intelligence consists of familiarity with the counting units for the basic building blocks of institutional research (that is, students, faculty, finances, and facilities). Intelligence at this level requires familiarity with the standard categories and definitions of basic terms (for example, part- or full-time, first-time, credit hours, contact hours, class status, race/ethnicity, personnel and salary grades). It also includes knowledge of basic counting rules and formulae (for example, for calculating the number of FTE students and faculty members, a building's inside net square feet, students' grade-point averages, student-faculty ratios, and costs per credit hour). Factual technical knowledge also includes familiarity with the structures, variable names, definitions and coding conventions, and creation and maintenance schedules of basic institutional data files (for example, admissions, registration, personnel, facilities).

Technical/analytical intelligence also refers to a broad array of methodological skills. Such skills include research design (for example, experimental, quasi-experimental, factorial, ex post facto, survey), sampling designs (for example, opportunity, purposive, simple random, stratified random, area, cluster), statistics (for example, bivariate procedures, factor analysis, multiple regression, structural modeling), measurement (for example, scaling, scale development, and the estimation of reliability and validity), and qualitative research methods (for example, interviewing, focus groups, participant observation, ethnography). Other "research" skills are also involved, including various techniques for enrollment projections and forecasting, faculty workload analysis, over- and understaffing analyses, student flow modeling, and assessment and program evaluation techniques. This category also includes library research skills, synthesizing abilities, oral and written communication skills, and knowledge of the institution's basic formal organizational and governance structures.

This category also consists of a wide variety of technical mainframe and personal computer skills. Mainframe skills include large database management and the use of resident application programs such as statistical packages (for example, SPSS, SAS), graphics packages, and electronic mail and file transfer. Personal computing skills include the use of word processing, electronic spreadsheets, graphics, database management, and decision and executive support system applications.

Tier 1 organizational intelligence is fundamental and foundational. Without the higher level forms of intelligence, however, it has little utility or value. By itself, it consists of data without information, processes without purposes, analyses without problems, and answers without questions.

Tier 2: Issues Intelligence. Issues intelligence involves most of the substantive problems on which technical and analytical intelligence is brought to bear. As with Tier 1 intelligence, it has both substantive and procedural dimensions. Substantive Tier 2 intelligence comprises knowledge of the major issues or decision areas that face institutions and the people who manage them. Such issues include the importance of, and rationale for, such managerial activities as enrollment goal setting; faculty workload analysis; resource allocation and reallocation; physical facilities planning, management, and maintenance; pricing (at private institutions); salary determination and equity issues; program and institutional planning; assessment, program evaluation, and institutional self-study; budget development and execution; and faculty evaluation. *Issues-intelligent* institutional researchers understand the major categories of problems confronting middle- and upper-level administrators in various parts of the institution (although the individual may not fully understand the complexity of those problems). For example, issues-intelligent institutional researchers are familiar not only with the technical procedures for developing enrollment projections but also with the processes and issues involved in enrollment *target* setting. They know not only how to read an account balance sheet and how to move funds around but also the budget development process and how it relates to annual and strategic planning activities.

Issues intelligence also involves an understanding of how institutions function and how decisions are made. Perhaps most important is an understanding and appreciation of the essentially political character of the decision areas listed above. If the technically/methodologically intelligent institutional researcher understands the formal organizational and governance structures, the issues intelligent institutional researcher also has a textbook-like understanding of informal power structures and reward systems and how to operate successfully within them. This form of generalized intelligence is reflected in one's knowledge of the importance and role of political persuasion, of compromise, of prior consultation with important opinion makers and organizational and governance units, and of personal and professional courtesy. It is a knowledge of how to work successfully with other people (both individually and in groups) to accomplish some goal.

It is important to note that these are general organizational and interpersonal skills. They are portable across institutional settings. They are necessary to the effective functioning of an institutional researcher, but they are not sufficient. Tier 3 intelligence, discussed below, is also necessary.

If technical/analytical intelligence by itself consists of processes without content and answers without questions, then issues intelligence, by itself, is content without processes and questions without the tools to answer them. It should be noted, however, that while Tier 2 intelligence implies the availability or presence of Tier 1 intelligence, the reverse is not the case. In the typical development of the institutional researcher, Tier 1 intelligence precedes Tier 2 intelligence, although such is not invariably the case.

Tier 3: Contextual Intelligence. Contextual intelligence involves understanding the culture both of higher education in general and of the particular campus where the institutional researcher works. It is what Robert Pace has referred to as "the knowledge of what a college is and where it has come from." It includes an understanding of the institution's historical and philosophical evolution, faculty and organizational cultures, informal as well as formal campus political structures and codes, governance, decision-making processes, and customs. It includes knowledge of how business is done in *this* particular college or university and who the "key players" are in both organizational and governance units. It requires understanding of the values and attitudes of the people with whom one works at all levels of the organization, and an appreciation of and respect for the perspectives of students, faculty, administrators, trustees, parents, legislators, and governors. In this regard, contextual intelligence also entails a knowledge of the local, state, national, and international environments within which the institution must function and which both present it with opportunities and constrain what it can hope to accomplish or become.

This category of intelligence reflects organizational savvy and wisdom. It is the crowning form of organizational intelligence, dependent upon the other two tiers but lifting them out of a preoccupation with topically relevant data and specific analytical tools. It makes possible the prudent, intelligent, and illuminating application of technical and methodological intelligence to locally meaningful versions of general issues. It represents both content and methodologies tailored to a specific institutional setting where real people are preparing to make real decisions. It is the form of intelligence that earns institutional research and researchers legitimacy, trust, and respect.

The Nature of the Preparation Implied

Each of the three kinds of organizational intelligence described here implies particular and different kinds of preparation. Some of this preparation may involve formal (most likely) graduate coursework, while some of the necessary preparation probably must be experiential.

Some kinds of Tier 1 (technical/analytical) intelligence can be acquired on-the-job, while other kinds will require formal training. Certain kinds of substantive Tier 1 intelligence (for example, that having to do with local terms, definitions, counting rules, formulae, and knowledge of institutional databases) is probably best gained through experience at an institution, but such learning will be institution specific, and the breadth of the learning is likely to be dependent upon the quality of the institutional research operation in which it is learned. If on-the-job training is received at the hands of individuals who themselves learned on the job, the training is likely to be limited and parochial.

Other forms of substantive technical and analytical intelligence are probably best acquired in a formal course in institutional research and planning offered by most graduate programs in higher education. Such training can provide exposure to and explanation of various models and approaches to such standard institutional research practices as enrollment projections, student flow modeling, workload analysis, resource allocation, faculty evaluation, program evaluation, assessment, institutional self-study, budget development and analysis, academic program planning, and institutional strategic planning.

Methodological and analytical skills *can* be learned through self-instruction or experience, but such learning, again, is likely to be incomplete, limited to the knowledge of the "teacher," and potentially inaccurate or misleading depending upon the level of the instructor's analytical competence. Such preparation is more likely to be sound and complete when received in formal coursework in such areas as research design, measurement, sampling, statistics, and qualitative research methods, provided by a department of educational psychology, statistics, psychology, sociology, public administration, or anthropology.

Skill in oral and written expression must be developed through practice and over time, but courses in speech and technical writing can help and are available at many colleges and most universities. Computer skills are most likely to be learned through self-instruction (often with the aid of a computerized tutorial that accompanies many software applications), "short courses" offered by computing centers, trial and error, and the assistance of accomplished users of the software application one is trying to learn.

Coursework in all these areas, however, can take one only so far. The highest levels of research or analytical competence come only through experience in the application and adaptation of these methodological and technical tools.

If technical and analytical intelligence is developed primarily and most surely through formal coursework, issues intelligence (Tier 2) can probably be developed through either coursework or experience, or a mix of the two, although coursework is more likely to provide comprehensive coverage of the various issue areas as well as more formal examination and analysis of each. Issues intelligence might be acquired through a survey course (such as the institutional research and planning course outlined above), but the completeness of the coverage and the depth of analysis are unlikely to be totally satisfactory. Additional coursework would be advisable in such areas as the history and philosophy of higher education, curriculum design and change, program development, organizational analysis (including governance issues), financing of higher education, legal issues, and students and the impact of college on them. The essence of this type of intelligence is an understanding of the content and processes of higher education in America. It means, for example, an understanding that budget development is not simply a set of steps one follows mechanically to produce an estimate of the human, financial, and material resources an institution is likely to need in each fund category for the coming year. It means understanding that budget development is a highly political process, involving a wide variety of stakeholders, each with an agenda and degree of influence on institutional functioning. It means understanding that there are informal as well as formal power structures and that colleges and universities are neither collegial, bureaucratic, nor political organizations but a shifting mix of all three (Baldridge, 1971). Familiarity with such issues (although not necessarily a full understanding) and respect for them is more likely to be acquired through formal coursework than through on-the-job training.

Tier 3 (contextual) intelligence can be acquired *only* through on-the-job training. One cannot learn the culture and context of the institution in which one works from a book. There are, however, two exceptions to this rule: first, a strong case can be made for the value of reading a good history of one's institution as a means of coming to understand its historical origins, organizational and curricular evolution, customs and traditions, and much else that defines the institution and gives it a distinctive context and identity. Second, reading the institution's most recent reaccreditation self-study report can also be highly informative. More likely, however, contextual knowledge comes from working on a campus for a number of years. Understanding the context and culture of one's institution may be advanced by the kinds of coursework recommended for developing Tier 2 intelligence, but such coursework will be useful only insofar as it suggests the general kinds of issues and dynamics that one should look for and analyze as one comes to know and understand a particular institution. For example, a good general history of higher education (such as Rudolph, 1962; Brubacher and Rudy, 1968) will tell one little about a particular institution, but having read it, one can then examine the historical evolution of one's own college or university against the general historical backdrop of American higher education. Similarly, any of a hundred books on organizational theory and analysis in higher education will identify faculty members as critically important players in the organizational functioning of a college or university, but having read all of them, one will still know nothing of the local faculty and its culture.

Such contextual knowledge can be acquired passively simply through employment on a campus for several years. A good institutional researcher, however, will actively seek to acquire it. Developing a high level of contextual intelligence means not only reading the history of one's institution but also reading newspapers (local, institutional, and student), as well as the minutes of important governance bodies. It means engaging people who are long-time employees (the people with the "institutional memories") in ongoing conversations about what the institution was and is becoming. It means clearly understanding the formal organizational and governance structures of the institution, identifying individuals and groups who wield significant formal or informal power. It means identifying "opinion shakers," those who, by virtue of their rank, tenure, professional stature, or personality, are listened to when they speak. It means purposefully seeking regular contact and conversation with deans, department heads, and faculty members, as well as administrators in key offices (particularly the staff to senior administrators if one is not already close to those administrators themselves) as a means of staying on top of what is happening in the various quarters of the institution, keeping communication channels open, understanding the institution from their perspective, developing and maintaining a sensitivity to the problems others are facing, and building good interpersonal working relationships with the people who depend on institutional research and upon whom the institutional research function depends.

Conclusion

Institutional research, in this paper, is conceived of as institutional intelligence in three, mutually dependent but distinct forms. The first form (Tier 1) consists of a technical/analytical competence that is both substantive (for example, familiarity with terms, definitions, counting rules) and methodological (for example, knowledge of research designs, sampling, statistics, measurement, computing, and qualitative methods, as well as enrollment forecasting, workload analysis, instructional and program evaluation, and the like). This form of intelligence is foundational; by itself, however, it is of little value.

A second form (Tier 2) of organizational intelligence, issues intelligence, requires an understanding of the substantive problems confronting administrators and on which the technical/analytical intelligence is brought to bear. Such intelligence is also both substantive and procedural. Substantive intelligence in this tier involves familiarity with the major categories of institutional decision making (for example, enrollment goal setting, resource allocation, physical facilities planning and management, program and institutional planning and assessment). Procedural competence includes knowledge of such activities as the budget development process and its linkages with academic and facilities planning, varying models for faculty workload analysis, faculty resource allocation, and faculty evaluation. But the procedural knowledge in this tier is not merely technical but rather is conditioned by an appreciation of the essentially political character of these activities and an understanding of how they can be completed successfully with the least amount of internal institutional friction.

Tier 3, or contextual intelligence, requires an understanding not only of the culture and customs of higher education in general but also of the particular institution in which the institutional researcher serves. It is a "sense of the place," of what the institution has been, what it is, and what it is becoming or can become. At its base, it is a form of institutional wisdom, the crowning form of institutional intelligence, transcending both technical competence and general administrative understanding. Contextual intelligence gives both Tier 1 and Tier 2 intelligence particular value by marrying them in the service of a particular institution facing specific and occasionally idiosyncratic problems.

Finally, these three forms of organizational intelligence are mutually dependent and supportive: only in the presence of the other two is the value of any specific form of organizational intelligence fully realized. Moreover, all three forms of organizational intelligence are found in truly effective institutional research offices, and occasionally they are found in the same individual. More such offices and individuals are needed.

PATRICK T. TERENZINI is professor and senior scientist in the Center for the Study of Higher Education at Penn State University.

*A nationwide survey of 601 AIR members reveals
perceived levels of institutional research knowledge
and skills, how IR knowledge and skills are acquired,
and how they relate to perceptions of effectiveness.*

Knowledge, Skills, and Effectiveness in Institutional Research

*William E. Knight, Michael E. Moore,
Corby A. Coperthwaite*

Gaither, Nedwek, and Neal (1994) note that growing costs, reduced public confidence, and eroding state support for higher education are among the reasons for increased concern over accountability, quality, and productivity in academe. Internal and external pressures calling for the assessment of college student learning and development have been joined by concerns over the effectiveness of administrative offices and functions. Recent higher education conferences and publications abound with discussions of performance indicators, such as the National Benchmarking Project of the National Association of College and University Business Officers, the National Study of Instructional Costs and Productivity, and the Strategic Indicators Project of Peterson's Guides and the Association of Governing Boards.

The IR function has not evaded these concerns. Most of the regional accrediting associations now have strong provisions for institutional effectiveness in such administrative functions as institutional research. For example, the Commission on Colleges of the Southern Association of Colleges and Schools (1995) prescribes in its criteria on institutional effectiveness that "an institution must regularly evaluate the effectiveness of its institutional research process" (p. 20). Although institutional research has

This chapter is based on a paper presented by the authors at the Association for Institutional Research Forum, Boston, May 1995, and subsequently published in *Research on Higher Education*, 1997, *38*, 419–433. Address correspondence to William E. Knight, Office of Institutional Research, Bowling Green State University, 301 McFall Center, Bowling Green, OH 43403.

not yet been the subject of externally imposed empirical performance indicators, its effectiveness has been a subject of ongoing interest among its community of practitioners as well (Billups and DeLucia, 1990; Dressel, 1981; Fincher, 1978, 1985; Harrington, 1995; Hearn and Corcoran, 1988; Presley, 1990; Sheehan, 1980; Volkwein, 1990).

Given this context, it is surprising that few studies exist that explore the effectiveness of institutional research and the means by which it can be improved. Unfortunately, most conference sessions about improving effectiveness tend to be based on the experiences of one or more individuals; they do not result from a systematic study of practitioners in the field.

One exception to this paucity of empirical research is a study by Huntington and Clagett (1991), which employed a national survey to explore institutional researchers' concerns about effectiveness and productivity. The biggest obstacles to increasing the effectiveness of these researchers' offices were inadequate staff size and expertise, campus leaders' lack of appreciation for data and research, inadequate technical resources, researchers' lack of access to decision makers, external reporting demands and (a related barrier) lack of time, researchers' not being seen as part of the institution's leadership team, insufficient identification of issues, and campus politics. Although many of the ideas proposed by survey respondents for increasing IR office productivity were related to resources ("add more staff," for example), the survey results also frequently cited skill training for IR staff, "early identification of key issues by management," and "regular communication with top management" as possible means for institutional researchers to overcome obstacles to their effectiveness.

Terenzini (1993) approached the issue of IR effectiveness in terms of the requisite professional characteristics of effective institutional researchers. He drew on numerous sources to articulate the three tiers of *organizational intelligence,* including technical/analytical intelligence, issues intelligence, and contextual intelligence (see Chapter Two for a more complete description). Terenzini's ideas about the knowledge and skills that IR professionals need to be fully effective in their jobs seem eminently logical and are in accordance with established principles of management and human resource development. However, they have not been empirically validated, either in terms of the existence and interrelationships of these types of knowledge and skills among practitioners or in terms of the relationship between them and indicators of effectiveness. This is the purpose of the current study. The specific research questions are

1. To what extent do IR professionals possess the three types of knowledge and skills proposed by Terenzini?
2. To what extent do these skills cluster into factors that conform to those proposed by Terenzini?
3. How do the experiences and activities of institutional research professionals predict or explain the degree to which they report having these types of knowledge and skills?

4. How do the knowledge and skills of institutional research professionals and their experiences and activities predict or explain their self-
   reported effectiveness?

Methodology

Surveys were mailed to Association for Institutional Research (AIR) members and 695 were returned (a response rate of 58.5 percent). The profile of
the participants was quite similar to that of the respondents to a recent AIR
membership survey (Lindquist, 1995a, 1995b); the percentages of participants by categories of experience in institutional research, institutional type,
highest academic degree, and reporting relationship never varied between
the two surveys by more than 5 percent.

Data were collected by means of a survey developed specifically for this
study. The first portion of the survey asked participants about their education, experiences, and activities, items Terenzini (1993) suggested were
related to IR intelligence. The top twenty of these items include job title,
years of experience, reporting relationships, educational level, staff size, institution type, educational discipline, and source of IR skills, among others.

The second part of the survey included items related to IR knowledge
and skills. These were developed from the full set of examples of the three
tiers of organizational intelligence articulated by Terenzini. These items are
listed in Table 3.1.

The last part of the survey requested that participants rate their overall effectiveness as IR professionals, using a five-point scale ranging from
"very effective" to "very ineffective." As no specific, broadly recognized measure of IR effectiveness appears in the literature, this single-item, self-
reported measure was the only means readily available to serve as a
dependent variable in the analyses.

Results

The study examines four research questions about IR knowledge and skills:

- Do IR professionals possess the three types of intelligence identified by
  Terenzini?
- Can the three types of intelligence be verified empirically?
- Do the experiences and activities of IR professionals predict their skills?
- Do IR skills and backgrounds predict effectiveness?

IR Knowledge and Skills. In response to the first research question,
participants said they possessed to a large extent the examples of technical/
analytical and issues knowledge and skills posed by Terenzini. To a lesser
extent they reported having the contextual knowledge Terenzini described.
Table 3.1 lists twenty-one of the thirty-four items on the survey. They are
the items most frequently cited by respondents and they are the strongest

Table 3.1. Factor Analysis Results of IR Knowledge and Skill Items

Items	1	2	3	4	5	h^2
			Factors			
Written communication skills (79 percent)	.85	.10	.09	.21	−.05	.78
Knowledge and skills in data presentation and reporting (81 percent)	.85	.06	.05	.18	.13	.78
Knowledge of how to work successfully with other people (79 percent)	.82	.17	.07	.20	−.02	.74
Familiarity with standard variable categories and definitions (81 percent)	.82	.07	.21.	−.06	.25	.79
Knowledge of basic counting rules and formulae (78 percent)	.79	.08	.24	−.08	.29	.77
Oral communication skills (70 percent)	.78	.12	.08	.26	−.07	.69
Knowledge of organizational and governance structures in general (72 percent)	.75	.22	.25	.08	.00	.68
Familiarity with the structures, definitions, and so forth of institutional data files (70 percent)	.69	.05	.19	−.08	.33	.63
Knowledge and skills with respect to computer application software (66 percent)	.68	−.07	.01	−.03	.24	.53
Knowledge of the need for prior consultation with important opinion makers (70 percent)	.67	.27	.30	.22	−.09	.66
Library research skills (57 percent)	.63	.08	.01	.36	.00	.54
Knowledge of the local community political environment and how it affects the institution (41 percent)	.13	.85	.06	.08	.00	.75
Knowledge of the state political environment and how it affects the institution (42 percent)	.15	.83	.12	.01	.10	.74
Knowledge of the perspectives, values, and attitudes of important legislators (28 percent)	−.13	.78	.13	.10	.19	.68
Knowledge of the national political environment and how it affects the institution (35 percent)	.14	.72	.13	.12	.11	.58
Knowledge of the importance of and rationale for faculty workload analysis (49 percent)	.19	.17	.82	.04	.29	.82
Knowledge of the importance of and rationale for salary equity studies (46 percent)	.15	.16	.80	.08	.20	.73
Technical knowledge and skills in instructional evaluation (31 percent)	−.12	.08	.22	.78	.15	.70
Technical knowledge and skills in assessment and program evaluation techniques (50 percent)	.33	.11	.12	.72	.15	.67
Technical knowledge and skills in enrollment forecasting (41 percent)	.16	.15	.25	.14	.77	.72
Technical knowledge and skills in student flow modeling (38 percent)	.00	.10	.31	.18	.72	.65

Note: Percentages in parentheses indicate participants who agreed or strongly agreed that they possess each type of knowledge or skill. Factor 1 = general IR knowledge and skills; Factor 2 = knowledge of the external political environment; Factor 3 = faculty-related IR knowledge; Factor 4 = technical knowledge and skills in assessment and instructional evaluation; Factor 5 = technical knowledge and skills in enrollment management research.

contributors to the factor analysis. The parentheses after each item show the percentage of participants who agreed or strongly agreed that they possessed each of the types of knowledge and skills listed.

A majority of the responding institutional researchers agreed or strongly agreed that they had a strong grasp of ten of the sixteen indicators of technical/analytical knowledge and skills. Participants were most likely to agree that they were knowledgeable about standard variable categories and definitions, data presentation and reporting, and basic counting rules and formulae and that they possessed strong written communication skills. They were least likely to agree that they possessed technical knowledge and skills in instructional evaluation and student flow modeling.

Similarly, a majority of the participants felt they strongly possessed seven of the nine examples of issues knowledge suggested by Terenzini. They reported being most knowledgeable about how to work successfully with other people, the need for prior consultation with important opinion makers, and the importance of and rationale for institutional self-study. They were least knowledgeable about the importance of and rationale for salary equity studies and faculty workload analysis.

Finally, a majority of IR practitioners responding to the survey purported to strongly possess about one-half of the contextual knowledge items. They were most familiar with the perspectives, values, and attitudes of campus executives and the history and unique characteristics of their institutions. They were least familiar with the perspectives, values, and attitudes of legislators who are important to their institutions and with the national political environment and how it affects their college or university.

Factor Analysis Results. The second research question was addressed by performing a factor analysis on the thirty-four IR knowledge and skill items listed in the survey. Principal components extraction was used with varimax rotation. Factor loadings, communalities (h^2), and percentages of variance for the principal factors are shown in Table 3.1. Items are ordered and grouped by size of loadings to facilitate interpretation. Boxes in the table indicate the items associated with each factor. The thirteen items that loaded at .40 or above on more than one factor are excluded from the table.

Five factors explain 67 percent of the total variance. Factor 1, which explains 41 percent of the total variance, is interpreted and titled as *general IR knowledge and skills.* Eleven items, nine of the examples of technical/analytical knowledge and skills suggested by Terenzini and two examples of issues knowledge and skills, show high loadings on this factor. Factor 2, *knowledge of the external political environment,* explains 10 percent of the total variance and comprises four items dealing with the local community, state, and national political environment and with the perspectives of legislators important to the institution. This factor corresponds to a portion of Terenzini's examples of contextual knowledge and skills; interestingly, only the external, not the internal, context is represented in the factor. Factor 3, *faculty-related IR knowledge*, accounts for 7 percent of the total variance and reflects knowledge of the importance of and rationale for faculty workload analysis and salary equity studies. Both of the items for this factor fall within Terenzini's examples of issues knowledge and skills. Factor 4 represents *technical knowledge and skills in assessment and instructional evaluation* and explains 5 percent of the total variance. These items are examples of technical/ analytical knowledge and skills. Factor 5, *technical knowledge and skills in enrollment management research*, accounts for 4 percent of the total variance, and these items are also examples of technical/analytical knowledge and skills.

Relationships Between Participants' Experiences and Activities and Their IR Knowledge and Skills. According to these results, only one factor (general IR knowledge and skills) represents a substantial number of knowledge and skill items (eleven) possessed by a large number of participants, and only this factor explains a substantial amount of the total variance (41 percent). Therefore a summed scale score (coefficient alpha = .94) of the items encompassing this factor contributes the one and only dependent variable. All the participant experiences and activities served as independent variables. Table 3.2 shows that although the number of years participants were employed in IR and the number of courses they completed in planning are significantly related to the dependent variable, these characteristics account for only 3 percent of its variance. None of the other background characteristics (for example, educational background, hours per week engaged in various activities, job title, type of institution where employed) served as significant predictors of general IR knowledge and skills.

The inability of educational background to predict the extent to which participants possessed technical skills is perhaps explained by the fact that on-the-job training was viewed as a greater contributor to skills acquisition than was coursework. The significance of the number of courses taken in planning may be attributed to the fact that such courses are available in a wide variety of graduate programs (for example, business and the social sciences), they are not available solely to individuals with a higher education administration background.

Perceptions of Effectiveness. In response to the fourth research question, stepwise multiple regression analysis examines the relationship between the self-reported effectiveness of institutional researchers, their professional knowledge and skills, and their experiences and activities. Table 3.3 shows that participants who have been employed in the field for a greater number of years, those holding the doctoral degree, those who are associate directors of institutional research, and those who report directly to their institution's president are more likely to consider themselves effective. Those who held a bachelor's degree as their highest degree, whose highest degree was in the field of education, and who had a greater level of general IR knowledge and skills were less likely to consider themselves

Table 3.2. Summary of Stepwise Regression Analysis for General IR Knowledge and Skills

Independent Variable	B	SE B	β
Years employed in institutional research	0.16	0.06	.12**
Number of graduate courses: planning	1.09	0.43	.11*

Note: $R^2 = .03$. The dependent variable is the general IR knowledge and skills factor.
*$p < .05$; **$p < .01$.

Table 3.3. Summary of Stepwise Regression Analysis for IR Effectiveness

Variable	B	SE B	β
Years employed in institutional research	.02	0.01	.19**
Highest degree: doctoral	.25	0.06	.11**
Title: associate director	.32	0.13	.10*
Reports to president	.15	0.07	.09*
Highest degree: bachelor's	−.28	0.11	−.12**
Highest degree field: education	−.21	0.08	−.11*
General IR knowledge and skills	−.01	0.00	−.11*

Note: $R^2 = .17$.
*$p < .05$; **$p < .001$.

effective. These seven variables accounted for only 17 percent of the variance in self-reported effectiveness.

Discussion

This study developed survey items reflecting Terenzini's three tiers of organizational intelligence. These items do not constitute a comprehensive taxonomy, and other specific IR knowledge and skills could probably be identified. (For example, knowledge and skills in using the World Wide Web for institutional research and knowledge of data warehousing and geodemography are recently developed examples of types of organizational intelligence not accounted for by Terenzini.) The survey was sent to a large proportion of the national AIR membership and a representative 58 percent responded. The most serious limitation of the current study is the single item of self-reported effectiveness. As noted earlier, however, no other comprehensive, broadly recognized measure appears to be available at this time.

Within these constraints we do provide some interesting conclusions for those interested in the professional development of institutional researchers. Most of the study respondents believe that they possess the examples of technical/analytical and issues intelligence articulated by Teren-zini. They believe they possess to a lesser extent the examples of contextual intelligence. Many of Terenzini's examples of technical/analytical intelligence are interrelated in terms of a general IR knowledge and skills factor, but additional examples of organizational intelligence are associated with other distinct factors. In all, we found five factors rather than three, but the largest amount of variance in the survey items is explained by a global factor reflecting general IR knowledge and skills. In sum, only two variables (years employed in institutional research and number of courses completed in planning) are related to general IR knowledge and skills (R^2 = .03), and only longevity, type and field of participant's highest degree, general IR knowledge and skills, being an associate director, and reporting directly to the president significantly predicted self-reported effectiveness (R^2 = .17). Thus the goals of the study were only partially achieved.

The existence of IR knowledge and skills factors distinct from the general factor suggests that there are separate areas of IR ability (for example, knowledge and skills in outcomes assessment, in faculty research, and in enrollment management research) that are not exhibited by (or perhaps needed by) all institutional researchers. The relationship between IR knowl-edge and skills in general and essentially nothing but longevity suggests that no specific educational or experiential background is requisite for these general abilities. The finding that 88 percent of the participants reported that on-the-job experience was their most important source of professional knowledge and skills suggests that experience may be a necessary, perhaps even a vital source of general IR knowledge and skills.

The paucity of variables related to IR effectiveness again suggests that few specific experiences seem requisite for self-rated effectiveness. The rela-tionship between effectiveness and being an associate director of insti-tutional research (especially because none of the other education and experience variables were substantially correlated with being an associate director) remains unexplained. The negative relationship between effec-tiveness and the general knowledge and skills factor suggests that general knowledge and skills may be a necessary but not sufficient condition for effectiveness. In order to be truly effective, in the broad sense, institutional researchers may need contextual as well as the more basic types of knowl-edge and skills.

These conclusions suggest that a quantitative study focusing on the rela-tionships between global effectiveness and preselected examples of knowl-edge, skills, and experiences may simply not be adequate to the goal of providing meaningful suggestions for improving institutional research. The authors' own experiences, Fincher's (1978) and Hearn and Corcoran's (1988) discussions about successful institutional research, and a logical extension of Terenzini's thesis of contextual intelligence to the idea of *contextual effec-tiveness* all lead to one conclusion. The effectiveness of institutional research can perhaps be evaluated only relative to both the capabilities, experiences, and orientation of the institutional researcher and the expectations, experiences, orientation toward information and rational decision making, and personalities of the institutional leadership. The institutional researcher whose tasks are limited to responding to external surveys and carrying out the annual student satisfaction survey or faculty salary study might (quite correctly) feel that he or she is very effective and possesses the requisite knowledge and skills for these tasks. Moreover, these circumstances and thus IR portfolios may differ from campus to campus, making generalizations like those attempted in this study difficult.

If this scenario represents the ways in which institutional research may or may not be viewed as effective and the ways in which the knowledge and skills of its practitioners may or may not be perceived as adequate, then it seems that further inquiry into this topic cannot be accomplished through use of a descriptive survey of a large number of practitioners. Further investigation may call for multiple detailed case studies designed to promote better understanding of the congruence between institutional decision support processes and the perceived role and effectiveness of institutional research.

WILLIAM E. KNIGHT is director of planning and institutional research at Bowling Green State University.

MICHAEL E. MOORE is director of institutional research at Georgia State University.

CORBY A. COPERTHWAITE is director of institutional research at Manchester Community-Technical College.

4

AIR member surveys from the past two decades tell us much about who we are, where we work, and what we do, and also show some areas of change.

A Profile of Institutional Researchers from AIR National Membership Surveys

Sarah B. Lindquist

Research for this chapter uncovered five national surveys of the Association for Institutional Research (AIR) membership that were conducted within the last two decades and that included items that could be used to develop a profile of the personal and organizational characteristics of individuals in our profession. These surveys include the 1981 and 1988 surveys of the professional development needs of the membership (Reichard, 1981, 1982a, 1982b; Endo and others, 1988; Endo, 1989), the 1994 and 1998 membership surveys (Lindquist, 1995a, 1995b; Noble, 1999), and the 1995 survey of institutional research knowledge and skills (Knight, Moore, and Coperthwaite, 1997). In addition, information from the 1992, 1994, 1996, and 1998 AIR Forum evaluations (AIR Forum Evaluation Committee, 1994, 1998), the 1989 AIR Factbook (Sharp, 1989), and the 1998 AIR Executive Office member database (June 30, 1998; $n = 2,905$) were examined when possible and relevant. An overview of the scope of each survey and forum evaluation and of the number of respondents for each is given in Table 4.1. Although the membership of AIR reflects a substantial proportion of individuals in the profession, we know that many practicing institutional researchers do not belong to AIR, and they may reflect a slightly different profile than those who do join AIR.

Who Are We?

Table 4.2 highlights survey information on the number of years respondents have been working in institutional research or related fields. Interestingly, except on the 1988 survey, about one-third of those in each year report that

Table 4.1. Scope of AIR National Membership Surveys and Forum Evaluations and Number of Survey Respondents

	1981 Professional Development Needs Survey	1988 Professional Development Needs Survey	1992 Atlanta Forum Evaluation	1994 Membership Survey	1994 New Orleans Forum Evaluation	1995 by Knight, Moore, and Coperthwaite	1996 Albuquerque Forum Evaluation	1998 Membership Survey	1998 Minneapolis Forum Evaluation
Scope	All AIR members (1,765)	All AIR members (1,800)	Forum Awards Luncheon participants	All 1994–95 AIR members and those who had not renewed from the previous year (2,688)	Forum Awards Luncheon participants	All AIR members with titles associated with IR (1,234)	Forum Awards Luncheon participants	All 1998–99 AIR members (2,257)	Forum Awards Luncheon participants
Number of respondents	674	902	458	1,252	459	601	483	941	464

Table 4.2. AIR Members' Years of Experience in Institutional Research

1981 Professional Needs Survey		1988 Professional Needs Survey		1992 Forum Evaluation		1994 Membership Survey		1994 Forum Evaluation	
1–4	27%	0–2	20%	0–1	11%	1–5	32%	0–1	7%
5–8	29	3–5	20	2–5	25	6–10	28	2–5	27
9–12	22	6–9	18	6–10	24	11–15	17	6–10	27
13+	17	9–14	23	11–20	30	16–20	12	11–20	27
		15+	20	20+	10	20+	11	21+	13

1995 Survey by Knight, Moore, and Coperthwaite		1996 Forum Evaluation		1998 Membership Survey		1998 Forum Evaluation	
Median	7	0–1	8%	0–1	7%	0–1	9%
Range	1–35	2–5	24	2–4	24	2–5	23
		6–10	24	5–9	24	6–10	25
		11–20	32	10–14	19	11–20	31
		20+	12	15–19	14	20+	12
				20+	14		

they have five or fewer years of experience. About two-thirds have six or more years in the profession, 40 percent indicate that they have eleven or more years, and one out of ten is above the twenty-year mark. Thus many appear to be new to the profession and many appear to select institutional research as a career field rather than as a transitional occupation.

Institutional researchers are generally well educated, judging by their degrees. About half have been awarded doctoral degrees and about 40 percent have earned master's degrees. Institutional researchers are a diverse group with academic degrees from a variety of disciplines. Most institutional researchers have received their degrees in education (about 40 percent) or the social sciences (about 30 percent), a category that includes humanities and fine arts. About 10 to 15 percent of those in the profession have backgrounds in the physical sciences, including mathematics and computer science, and about 10 to 15 percent have degrees in business.

Three sources offered information on the gender of institutional researchers: the 1989 AIR Factbook, the 1994 AIR Membership Survey, and the 1998 AIR member database. The 1989 AIR Factbook reported that 75 percent of the membership was male in the 1980–81 academic year and 63 percent was male in the 1987–88 year. Respondents to the 1994 Membership Survey were 54 percent male and 46 percent female. Of the over twenty-nine hundred AIR members recorded in the 1998 member database, 52 percent were male and 48 percent female. It appears that more women have moved into the institutional research field over the years.

The 1994 Membership Survey and the 1998 AIR member database also contain information on the ethnicity and age of institutional researchers. In the 1994 survey, 88 percent of the respondents reported that they were white (non-Hispanic), 4 percent were African American, 3 percent Asian American or Pacific Islander, 3 percent Hispanic, and 1 percent American Indian or Alaskan Native, and 2 percent belonged to various "other" groups. The data from the 1998 member database show a little more diversity with 86 percent of the members indicating that they were white/Caucasian, 5 percent African American, 5 percent Asian American or Pacific Islander, 3 percent Hispanic, 1 percent American Indian or Alaskan Native, and 2 percent "other."

The mean age of respondents was forty-six in the 1994 Membership Survey and forty-eight in the 1998 member database. In the 1994 survey, 25 percent were in their twenties and thirties, 43 percent in their forties, and 33 percent fifty or older. In the 1998 member database, 26 percent were in their thirties or younger, 36 percent of the members were in their forties, and 38 percent fifty or older. This age information supports the premise that institutional research is a field that has a healthy number of young entrants but also has a substantial proportion of practitioners who have entered the field for the long term.

Where Do We Work?

AIR membership surveys and forum evaluations indicate that about two-thirds of institutional researchers are employed at four-year colleges or universities (see Table 4.3). About one-fifth are working at two-year colleges. Other major places of employment include government agencies or system offices (4 to 10 percent); graduate, professional, or upper-division institutions (3–5 percent); and private business (1 to 3 percent). Most institutional researchers are associated with public institutions or organizations (over 70 percent). These percentages have been fairly stable over the years. The 1998 AIR member database provides some greater refinement of the types of institutions in which we work, with 26 percent of members employed at research universities; 9 percent at doctoral degree granting universities; 22 percent at comprehensive colleges and universities; 10 percent at liberal arts colleges; 20 percent at two-year community, junior, and technical colleges, 4 percent at other institutions, and 10 percent not employed by a postsecondary institution.

Members of our profession are well represented at colleges and universities of all sizes. About 20 to 25 percent are employed at small institutions, with five thousand or fewer students. Approximately 30 to 45 percent are working at moderate-size institutions, with five thousand to twenty thousand students. And about 25 to 35 percent are found at large institutions, with over twenty thousand students.

Institutional researchers are working in offices of varying sizes too. Most are employed in offices that can be characterized as one-person or

Table 4.3. Organizational Characteristics of AIR Members' Employers

	1981 Professional Development Needs Survey	1988 Professional Development Needs Survey	1992 Atlanta Forum Evaluation	1994 Membership Survey	1994 New Orleans Forum Evaluation	1996 Albuquerque Forum Evaluation	1998 Minneapolis Forum Evaluation
Type of Employer							
Four-year college or university	67%	71%	67%	67%	69%	71%	66%
Two-year college	16	18	14	19	17	15	20
Graduate, professional, or upper-division institute	3		5	3	4	1	3
System office, government agency, or nonprofit organization	8	4	10	7	6	9	9
Business or consulting	2	3		1			
Other	4	4	3	4	3	4	2
Affiliation							
Public		70	72	70	77	78	75
Private		26	22	29	20	20	22
Does not apply		4	5	2	3	3	4
Student headcount							
0–2,000	11		7	10	8	8	5
2,000–5,000	14		16	15	12	11	14
5,000–10,000	16		14	19	17	16	17
10,000–20,000	17		31	23	26	30	28
20,000+	26		32	26	36	35	36
NA/no response	16			8			

small, that is, offices having two or fewer professional staff. About 20 to 25 percent are working in medium-size offices, with three or four professional staff, and about 20 percent are working in large offices, with five or more professional staff.

These surveys contain little information about where the IR office is located in the structure of an educational institution or to whom the office reports. Data from the 1994 Membership Survey indicate that about two-thirds of the respondents are located in departments in academic affairs or academic services divisions (38 percent) or in departments reporting to the president or chancellor (26 percent). Over 70 percent of those responding to the 1981 Professional Needs Survey said that the IR office reported directly to a vice president or to the president.

What Do We Do?

To say the least, institutional research is a complex field. Both John Muffo and Patrick Terenzini begin their chapters in this volume with discussions of how difficult it is to explain to people what institutional research is. The purpose of the *Primer on Institutional Research* (1987, 1992) is to introduce the more common activities and issues in which institutional researchers are engaged. A look at the primer's contents gives some insight into what institutional researchers do.

In the first edition of the primer (Muffo and McLaughlin, 1987), the topics included student retention, attrition, and flow studies; student needs assessment; program evaluation and self-study; budgeting and financial planning; economic impact studies; peer institutional studies; factbook preparation; and use of statistical software. The eleven "bread-and-butter" institutional research issues covered in the second edition (Whiteley, Porter, and Fenske, 1992) included student persistence, enrollment management, student impacts, faculty demand, faculty salaries, peer institutions, diversity, environmental scanning, Total Quality Management, academic program review, and cost analysis.

Is this really what we do in practice? The 1981 AIR Professional Development Needs Survey asked AIR members to identify from a 114-activity checklist those activities that had been performed by the member or his or her office in the past two years (Reichard, 1982a, discusses the results).

The 1981 survey indicates that the top ten activities of institutional research offices deal with (1) the analysis of student retention and attrition, (2) development of enrollment projections, (3) support of institutional-level planning processes, (4) factbook development, (5) analysis of instructional program credit-hour costs, (6) institutional self-study and accreditation, (7) management information systems, (8) use of statistical packages for planning and analysis, (9) external reporting needs, and (10) follow-up surveys of graduates. These activities were reported by at least 60 percent of institutional research offices.

Those activities reported in the 1981 AIR survey by members who were not employed in institutional research offices deal with (1) support of institutional-level planning processes, (2) implementation of planning processes, (3) development of enrollment projections, (4) management information systems, (5) analyses of instructional program credit hour costs, and (6) analyses of planning strategies and political approaches to planning. Reichard (1982) notes that AIR members employed in organizational settings other than IR offices seem to place a heavier emphasis on planning activities.

Since 1992, the AIR Forum evaluations have asked respondents to rate the relative importance of each of a number of institutional research topics to their professional role. This information can identify the areas that are demanding institutional researchers' attention. These topics and the percentage of respondents who rated each topic of high importance are shown in Table 4.4. The top four topics rated as highly important over the seven years covered by these forum evaluations are outcomes assessment, student persistence and retention, research design and analysis, and enrollment management. Moreover these four areas appear to have grown in importance during the 1990s. Enrollment management and related topics, such as retention and persistence, have received prominent coverage in the 1987 and 1992 primers on institutional research (Muffo and McLaughlin, 1987; Whiteley, Porter, and Fenske, 1992). In 1998, three new topics were considered highly important by over 60 percent of the respondents: accountability and performance indicators, technology issues, and information systems and data management. These three topics and four others in Table 4.4 received no attention in the two primers.

Another indicator of what is important in the practice of our profession is the perceived need for training or professional development in specific areas. Respondents to the 1981 Professional Needs Survey were asked to list the topics that they would most like to learn more about or receive training in. AIR members in the 1994 and 1998 Membership Surveys were asked to indicate their likelihood of attendance at workshops on particular topics. Table 4.5 summarizes the most frequently requested areas of training from these three surveys. Although topics like enrollment projection, data management, and statistics are consistently desired over the years, we see, over time, a topic shift away from the uses of microcomputers, market research, and financial analysis and toward performance indicators, benchmarking, assessment, and distance education.

In the 1988 Professional Needs Survey, respondents were asked to rate the importance of twenty-four topical areas and sixteen methodological and technical areas for their professional development. In the areas for professional growth, institutional data management ranked as the most important, followed by strategic planning, educational outcomes, student retention, and academic program review. The most highly rated among the methodological and technical areas were using microcomputers, using software

Table 4.4. AIR Members' Topics of High Importance to Their Professional Role

Topic	1992 Atlanta Forum Evaluation	1994 New Orleans Forum Evaluation	1996 Albuquerque Forum Evaluation	1998 Minneapolis Forum Evaluation
Outcomes assessment	53%	63%	60%	61%
Persistence and retention (P-1, P-2)	48	58	60	63
Research design and analysis	50	54	55	52
Enrollment management (P-1, P-2)	35	40	40	39
Management issues	42	43	42	32
Financial issues (P-1, P-2)	25	26	26	21
Faculty issues (P-2)	24	30	31	22
Minority and diversity issues (P-2)	25	24	23	19
Student affairs issues (P-1)	13	19	18	15
Accountability and performance indicators				71
Technology issues				63
Information systems and data management				63
Efficiency issues				36

P-1 = chapter topic in 1987 IR Primer
P-2 = chapter topic in 1992 IR Primer

Sources: P-1: chapter topic in Muffo and McLaughlin, 1987; P-2: chapter topic in Whiteley, Porter, and Fenske, 1992.

Table 4.5. AIR Members' Most Frequently Requested Areas of Professional Development

	1981 Professional Needs Survey	1994 Membership Survey	1998 Membership Survey
Focus of survey item	Topics members desired to learn more about or to receive training in	Workshops members were "likely" to attend	Topics on which members felt a "strong" or "moderate" need for additional training or information
Topic of training or workshop	Uses of microcomputers Developing enrollment projections Market research Financial analysis Uses of statistical packages Management information systems Database development, and management and control Policy analysis Statistics Analyzing student retention and attrition	Outcomes and institutional effectiveness assessment Research on students Enrollment projection and management Program review and evaluation Strategic planning Statistics for IR Information technology and resource management Survey research Policy analysis Data management and administration	Performance indicators Benchmarking and peer comparisons Enrollment projections Assessment development Faculty productivity Statistical methods Planning and organization Distance education Electronic data interchanges or exchanges Data management and administration

packages, conducting longitudinal tracking studies, applying strategic planning techniques, and using statistical methods.

In general, it appears that institutional researchers in the 1980s and 1990s are still engaged in similar activities and interested in similar topics. Institutional researchers from both decades and likely into the future have focused on student retention and other student research, enrollment management, data management and information systems, policy and budget analysis, academic program review and self-study, peer comparisons, factbook production, research design and analysis, and faculty studies. Areas that seem to have come into their own in the 1990s include strategic planning, Total Quality Management, outcomes assessment, institutional effectiveness, and technology.

Conclusion

This chapter presents a profile of institutional researchers based on AIR membership data. These personal and organizational characteristics may be used to develop what could be considered a *typical,* or *average,* member of our profession. This statistical individual is in his or her forties and has six to twenty years of experience in institutional research. He or she has earned a doctoral degree in education or the social sciences and is employed at a four-year public campus. This individual works in an office with two or fewer professional staff and which is located in the academic affairs division or under the president or chancellor. He or she generates data and conducts studies on myriad issues and activities encompassed by institutional research but most likely devotes substantial attention to assessment, retention, and enrollment management.

Of course there is no such thing as a typical institutional researcher. Perhaps what draws us to this profession is its diversity, not only in the characteristics of the people that it attracts but also in the wide array of activities and functions that it covers.

SARAH B. LINDQUIST is assistant dean of the Graduate College, Arizona State University.

5

Technology, demographics, emphasis on pedagogy, and national, regional, and state policy shifts are becoming forces in both the day-to-day activities and long-term goals of IR offices.

A Comparison of Findings from Regional Studies of Institutional Research Offices

John A. Muffo

In *A Primer on Institutional Research* (Muffo and McLaughlin, 1987), Gerry McLaughlin and I begin the introduction by discussing the difficulties of explaining to people outside the field what institutional research is. To the external community, faculty teach classes and administrators tell the faculty what to do (demonstrating the naive understanding of outsiders!). But a simple explanation of institutional research continues to allude us. In previous years I resorted to telling people that I worked with computers, and that seemed acceptable in most cases. At least I did not get many questions after that. Today everyone works with computers, so I am forced to mumble words like "data" and "analysis" and "reports," hoping that there are not too many follow-up questions.

The field has come a long way from the early days of student and space studies at a few places like the Universities of Minnesota and Illinois, where bookkeeping ledgers, slide rules, turn-of-the-century learning theory, and the youthful science of statistics (with all calculations done by hand) were state of the art (see Dressel, 1981, pp. 229–232). We have made much progress since the founding of the Association for Institutional Research in 1966, and the early years when the AIR Forums were attended by invitation only. Yet some basic questions remain: What is institutional research all about? What tools does it use? How is it practiced in various settings? What are the trends in the field? This volume addresses these questions, and this chapter contributes especially to suggesting answers to the last two.

Summary of Past Studies

Scholars have examined the knowledge and skills needed to be an effective institutional researcher (Terenzini, 1993), as well as the major difficulties and conflicts that emerge from serving in a wide range of roles and capacities (Volkwein, 1990). Survey results support the findings of both Terenzini and Volkwein and frequently note that IR work and attitudes toward the field are situational. "An institutional researcher's effectiveness can perhaps only be adequately evaluated relative to institutional culture and expectations and leaders, personalities and orientation toward decision making" (Knight, Moore, and Coperthwaite, 1997). Simply restated, you can be a bum one day and a hero the next without changing yourself but simply by outliving the current administration. That rings familiar to those of us who have been on the battle lines for a long time.

In the previous chapter Sarah Lindquist summarizes the results of several national surveys conducted by AIR. Although these surveys include responses from institutional researchers throughout North America, there are many institutional research practitioners in the United States and Canada who do not belong to AIR but who are active at regional and state levels. I found in the literature since 1990 six discussions of studies of institutional research as practiced in Canada and in the United States at regional and state levels.

Canada. The most recent published study of Canadian institutional research offices and their staffs is by Shale and Gomes (1990) and shows a pattern slightly different from that of past AIR studies and from that of the North American regional ones. The authors limited their research to major universities in Canada, so institutional diversity is more restricted than in most other studies of institutional research. (Some regional groups, such as Pacific Northwest AIR and Northeast AIR [NEAIR], include Canadian as well as U.S. members, but in both cases the vast majority of members are from the United States.)

As shown in Table 5.1, the twenty-seven Canadian institutions are rather large, public universities with IR offices exceeding five professional staff. Perhaps the most interesting aspect of the Shale and Gomes research is the extent to which institutional research in Canada is more focused on budgetary, budget planning, and related matters than it is in the U.S. regions and states. This can be seen in Table 5.1 by the low percentage of Canadian institutional research offices reporting to or through the academic vice president or president and the low percentage of offices headed by directors with doctoral degrees. In the United States it is small, two-year and four-year colleges that are most likely to have IR directors without a doctoral degree, as noted in other studies described below. A number of offices in Canada report that the shift toward budgetary matters has occurred in the last decade. Interestingly, a number of Canadian IR offices indicated an increased involvement in the major decision-making processes of their institutions because they had become increasingly more involved in budgeting and planning (Shale and Gomes, 1990, p. 4).

Table 5.1. Studies of Canadian and U.S. Regional and State IR Offices

Region	Year	Governance Split	Average Campus Size	Mean IR Size (Approximate FTE)	Administrative Reporting Area (percent)	Headed by Doctoral Degree Holder (%)	Dominant Tasks	Preferred Tasks
Canada (Shale and Gomes) n = 27	1990	Public university only	14,193	5.5	President = 15 Academic vice president = 11 Other = 74	15	Enrollment analysis Compiling statistics	NA
Northeast (Volkwein) n = 141	1990	51% Private 85% Four-year	3,300	1.3	President = 40 Academic vice president = 25 Other = 35	52	Enrollment management External reporting	NA
New England (Delaney) n = 127	1997	64% Private 74% Four-year	<2,000	1.0	President = 34 Academic vice president = 38 Other = 35	18	Enrollment analysis Institutional reporting	Enrollment management Academic studies
South (Harrington and Chen) n = 240	1995	75% Public 80% Four-year	10,477	4.5	President = 24 Academic vice president = 34 Other = 42	56	Institutional planning External reporting	Institutional planning Academic planning and analysis
Georgia (Harrington, Knight, and Christie) n = 54	1994	53% Public 51% Four-year	1,500–4,999 (Median range)	3.0	President = 55 Academic vice president = 27 Other = 18	37 (All IR staff)	National surveys Affirmative action reports	NA
Oklahoma (Hellman) n = 36	1998	58% Four-year	7,027 (Public only)	3.7	NA	38 (All IR staff)	NA	NA

The Northeast and New England. There have been two published studies in the Northeast (Volkwein, 1990; Delaney, 1997) with roughly similar conclusions—not surprising given the geographical overlap of the two groups surveyed (see Table 5.1).

The first published study of Northeast AIR members was conducted by Volkwein (1990). He found large variations among 141 institutional research offices in their staff size, academic backgrounds, organizational locations, and most frequent tasks. He notes that these findings are generally congruent with the single-institution Hearn and Corcoran (1988) case study revealing that campus arrangements for institutional research are subject to differing management styles, personalities, career paths, and administrative culture.

Volkwein found a very strong correlation (.73) between the size of the institution and the size of its IR office, with smaller offices being more likely to report to the president and larger offices being more likely to report to a vice president. Moreover, larger offices tend to have more highly trained and experienced staffs carrying out a more complex array of analytical tasks. Volkwein identified a core of IR tasks that are likely to be conducted by institutional researchers regardless of institution type and IR location in the hierarchy: enrollment management studies and projections, external reporting, and producing the campus factbook. IR tasks beyond this core tend to be influenced by organizational location. For example, IR offices reporting to academic affairs are more likely to undertake instructional analysis and faculty studies, whereas those reporting to finance and business are more likely to be involved in budget studies. Interestingly, although only one-third of the Northeast research staff possess a doctoral degree, more than half the reporting offices are headed by a director with an earned doctorate.

A more recent study of 127 campuses in New England (Delaney, 1997) confirms many of these findings. The New England study is dominated by small, private, four-year institutions with small IR offices, generally headed by a person with a master's degree (see Table 5.1). Delaney found strong relationships between "the institution's size and the scope of the institutional research function, . . . and the size and qualifications of the institutional research staff" (p. 1). Only in those few New England institutions with over five thousand students (9.3 percent of responding campuses) do most directors hold an earned doctoral degree. Like Volkwein, Delaney found that the greater the size of the institution and its IR office, the more likely the IR staff are to conduct analytical studies in addition to reporting descriptive statistics. Not surprisingly, enrollment management studies are the most frequently mentioned activities, with external reporting ranking second. When asked how they would like to spend their time, the respondents ranked academic studies (for example, academic program review, academic program evaluation, and outcomes assessment) just behind enrollment management in popularity.

The South. Harrington and Chen (1995) report a slightly different situation in the South, where larger public colleges and universities are more numerous than in the Northeast (see Table 5.1). Although Delaney's sample was 64 percent private college and university institutional researchers, of whom 60 percent worked in institutions of less than 2,000 students, three-fourths of Harrington and Chen's sample of 110 respondents from seventy different institutions in seventeen states worked at public institutions with a mean student FTE enrollment of 10,477. However, only 56.5 percent had doctoral degrees, a percentage similar to Volkwein's finding, and office location in the organization also reflected Volkwein's results. For example, those institutional researchers at the smallest places were the ones most likely to report to the president. Like their Northeast and New England colleagues, Southern AIR members report enrollment management (including retention and attrition studies and enrollment projections) and external reporting (including factbook development) to be at the top of their work agenda.

The greatest difference in activities is that the Southern AIR members rate outcomes assessment and institutional self-study roles higher than those in the Northern regions. At the time of the Volkwein survey, outcomes assessment was a major responsibility at almost half the NEAIR campuses, but it was that important at only a third of the New England campuses in Delaney's study. The greater assessment responsibility in the South may be due to a decade of requirements from the Southern Association of Colleges and Schools (SACS) to show evidence of outcomes assessment, along with the many state agencies in the South with accountability reporting requirements that emphasize outcomes assessment. Both these forces influence the large number of public institution researchers in the sample.

Only two state-focused studies, from Georgia and Oklahoma, appear in the recent literature. Unlike other studies described in this chapter, which focus on the office as the primary unit of measure, these two focus on individual practitioners (see Table 5.1). Nevertheless they yield information consistent with the regional studies.

Georgia. The study of Georgia institutional researchers by Harrington, Knight, and Christie (1994) reveals patterns similar to the regional studies: office size dependent on institutional size; more directors reporting to presidents, followed by academic vice presidents; heavy involvement in standardized reporting externally and internally and in attrition, retention, and enrollment management studies. A major finding is that "contrary to our expectations, professional variables appear to have less influence on the difficulty and complexity of tasks carried out [sic] in the institutional research offices, than do organizational variables" (p. 21). Stated another way, where you work has more to do with what you do than do your personal credentials.

Oklahoma. The study of Oklahoma institutional researchers focuses more on individual characteristics and less on organizational ones than the other studies mentioned here do, though it is consistent with the other studies where it makes organizational characteristics available (Hellman, 1998). The study identifies five factors important to institutional researchers: general knowledge and skills (fifteen items), external political environment (five items), faculty-related institutional research (three items), assessment and instructional evaluation (three items), and enrollment management research (two items). The obstacles to institutional research effectiveness sound familiar: demands for routine data, campus politics, leaders who do not want or use information, lack of researcher familiarity with methods, and a view that IR is not important, among others.

Future Prospects

These regional studies and my own assessment of the field lead me to draw certain conclusions. Certainly, some regional differences are likely to persist due to the different institutional makeup of the regions, with, for example, the majority of Northern colleges and universities continuing to be private and smaller than their counterparts in the rest of the United States. Nevertheless, there seems to be an evolving core of institutional research activities that most campuses have in common. As the field of institutional research matures, however, it is subject to the influences of strong external forces. Among these forces that will shape the future of IR are technology; demographics; emphasis on pedagogy; and national, regional, and state policy shifts.

Technology. Obviously, technology is having, and will continue to have, a tremendous impact on what we do. Those of us who can remember punch cards and mainframe systems matched with arcane computer programs are now confronted with desktop machines more powerful than the multimillion-dollar monsters of the past. And now we can use all this dedicated power (not just a few milliseconds here and there) with software that is increasingly user friendly. Now the difficulty is not producing stacks of statistical reports but interpreting them. It is becoming more common for people with limited statistical knowledge, for example, to produce mounds of numbers and Greek letters without the slightest idea of what it all means. As technology continues to improve, we may need to become data interpreters as much as data generators.

In particular, technology should help small offices operate efficiently without large numbers of people. Much of institutional research reporting, for example, is predetermined by the institution and not by the size of the institution, so the improvements and lower costs in technology should assist the smaller places. Technology should make more of an impact where there are more small, private colleges.

In the larger universities that predominant in the South, Midwest, and West, technology may well lead to further decentralization of institutional research and assessment. The access to and manipulation of data at the college and department level, so important to managers in tight fiscal environments, as noted by Hearn and Corcoran (1988), now can be done fairly easily and cheaply at the unit level, possibly leading to more decentralization of traditional institutional research functions. Such a trend is less likely at smaller colleges and universities, where the need and resources for data manipulation are at a higher level in the organization.

Demographics. One of the real driving forces for institutional research from its very inception has been demographics, which drive enrollments, which drive income and consequently institutional survival. Demographic patterns differ by region and hence will lead institutional researchers to emphasize different areas of study depending on where they work. Both Volkwein (1990) and Delaney (1997) report that enrollment management is a dominant IR activity in NEAIR and New England, as might be expected in an area where population is not growing as fast as in, for instance, the West. Accommodating thousands of new students at minimal cost—and admissions selectivity—is more likely to be a future concern in states like California and Florida. Institutional researchers and assessment professionals in regions of high growth are more likely to be studying the efficacy of off-campus programs delivered by multiple means. The reporting challenges alone should be enough to keep many of us busy.

Demographics also can affect other issues, such as changing student racial and ethnic numbers and religious mixes as well as shifting preparedness for college study. Increased rates of divorce and complex family profiles can present additional student counseling and financial aid challenges. Some institutions have major programs aimed at the elderly, especially in a campus's underutilized summer months. One need only to project demographic trends ahead a few years to see where institutional researchers are likely to be directed as they collect information for decision makers. The impact of these demographic trends certainly varies by region, in other parts of the world as well as in North America.

Emphasis on Pedagogy. Many of the early institutional research studies, as stated previously, focused on student retention and achievement. The outcomes assessment movement, in which institutional research has played a key role, has brought increased attention back to student learning. The tools available today are far better than before. Not only is the technology for assessing student learning more developed, but a larger body of knowledge exists on which to build. The challenges are greater too, however. There are not only branch campuses now but also programs delivered by correspondence, by television, and over the Internet, and in future years via mechanisms that we have yet to dream about. The impact on the enterprise called higher education is likely to be tremendous.

Until recently the emphasis on outcomes assessment has been strongest in the South and in certain academic disciplines where it has served accreditation purposes. This appears to be changing, with most regions now emphasizing such assessment in accreditation. Given the pressures from the federal government, it is likely that a de facto minimum standard is evolving nationally, though some regional differences may persist.

National, Regional, and State Policy Shifts. Given that many institutional researchers spend a lot of their time in reporting to national public and private organizations and to state public bodies, it does seem reasonable to assume that tasks will continue to shift along with the interests of policymakers. Recent examples of such reporting include the Student Right to Know legislation at the federal level in the United States and various performance indicator reports in many states.

Though some regional policy differences arise from time to time, the recent trends seem to be more state specific than regional. Performance indicator reporting is important in some states—for example, South Carolina, Colorado, and Virginia. It appears that state legislative and executive officers and the various governing and coordinating board members and staffs have strong information sharing networks (also assisted by technology). As a consequence, ideas are shared quickly across North America and internationally, with implementation being more dependent on state and provincial politics and personalities than on regional trends. The best source of information for the hard-pressed institutional researcher may be across the continent rather than in a bordering state or province.

Conclusion

The studies of different areas of North America do reveal some differences among institutional researchers and their offices based primarily on institutional size, governance (for example, private versus public), and accreditation areas of emphasis. Currently U.S. regional accreditation standards appear to be becoming more similar across regions, due to federal government regulations and to other national and international pressures that limit differences. It may well be then that institutional size and governance may be the most important factors distinguishing institutions, and these factors are only minimally affected by geography.

Technology has shrunk the world to the extent that regionalism will mean less and less to higher education, including institutional research, in the future. Small, private, religious or nonsectarian colleges are going to have more in common with their cross-continent counterparts in many cases than with the public university across town. Similarly, the institutional research agenda at a public institution will be driven by the latest accountability craze in the state or provincial capital, perhaps one picked by a politician while attending a conference three thousand miles away.

This is not to imply that state, provincial, and regional professional meetings will become irrelevant. On the contrary, communication between colleagues becomes even more important in an era of a quick and easy flow of ideas among those with whom we interact. What it does imply, however, is that sharing across the continent will increase in importance beyond its current level, so that all of us can have the supporting knowledge we need to do our jobs.

The world is only going to get more complex; no one person can know all that is necessary to get the job done. So it is more important than ever that we support each other with the latest information, within and across governmental boundaries. State, provincial, and regional organizations, as well as the Association for Institutional Research and other national and international organizations, will survive and prosper if they assist with such needs and may disappear if they do not.

JOHN A. MUFFO is director of the academic assessment program at Virginia Tech.

6

This chapter critiques some common assumptions about the rationality or irrationality of organizational behavior and suggests that decision making occurs in a complex context that successful IR offices recognize and work with.

Emerging Perspectives on Organizational Behavior: Implications for Institutional Researchers

Frank A. Schmidtlein

Over time, concepts of higher education governance practices and structures evolve and change, thereby influencing organizational processes and practices. To be most effective, institutional researchers should be aware of current theoretical perspectives on organizational behavior and, perhaps more important, of the theories and normative assumptions held by institutional policymakers. This chapter provides a review of recent changes in some commonly held assumptions about the character of organizations and an examination of their implications for institutional researchers.

The Character and Role of Organizational Theories

Kuhn's highly influential *The Structure of Scientific Revolutions* (1970) describes how changes in the theoretical assumptions, or *paradigms*, underlying scientific research have "revolutionized" various fields of inquiry. Similarly, as new theories on organizational behavior have emerged, new management concepts, techniques, and processes based on these theories have gained popularity. Concepts of *rational decision making* and *bureaucracy*, for example, have led to processes such as program planning and budgeting systems (PPBS); program evaluation and review technique (PERT), quality circles, strategic planning, and Total Quality Management (TQM).

The persistence of new techniques and processes depends on the degree to which their supporting theories adequately reflect organizational reality. For example, if a process fails to accommodate the time and information constraints affecting a chief executive's role, it will not work, as Hunt (1966) pointed out in "Fallacy of the One Big Brain." Allen and Chaffee (1981) noted the frequent coming and going of "management fads" in higher education.

Often organizations implement only the facade, not the substance, of a theoretically questionable process. A classic example of this phenomenon was the development and demise of program planning and budgeting systems in the United States. In the opinion of many critics, such as Lindblom (1959), Wildavsky (1966)), Balderston and Weathersby (1972), and Schmidtlein (1983), the theoretical assumptions behind this process were flawed. Consequently, after a wave of enthusiasm and widespread attempts at adoption, the process was found wanting in various respects and eventually was largely abandoned even though one can see remnants of its form in some current budget processes. A budget process that rests on similar theoretical assumptions, *performance funding,* currently is gaining a considerable number of advocates.

Institutional researchers operate on the basis of both implicit and explicit theories about organizational behavior. The extent to which their advice is heeded and their efforts contribute to policy and decisions largely depends on whether the assumptions behind their research and conclusions correspond to institutional realities and institutional leaders' organizational assumptions. If the theoretical assumptions of institutional research (IR) staff differ significantly from those of campus leaders, then these leaders will tend to ignore IR advice, despite its intrinsic value. Consequently, the continuing success of institutional researchers requires a sensitivity to the theories and assumptions about institutional behavior held by those IR serves as well as to the theories found in the literature and based on scholarship, research, and practical experience.

The character of the tension between an institutional researcher's theoretical perspectives on institutional policy and practices and the perspectives of those using his or her research has important implications. If the differences are viewed as ones of principle, then accommodation can be difficult. If compromises are made, researchers are left with a belief that they have "sold out" or have engaged in a futile enterprise. In such cases institutional researchers may inaccurately view politics, defined pejoratively, as having superseded rationality in establishing policy and practices. In contrast, when theoretical differences are seen as pragmatic issues that are subject to modification through new insights, negotiation, and compromise, then divergent points of view can be accommodated to a greater extent.

One common theoretical difference between institutional research staff and those they serve is whether their research is a cost-effective way to obtain information relevant to decisions. An institutional researcher may not be able to alter a superior's unfavorable perspectives but should at least be able to understand the theoretical basis for the differing points of view.

Clearer understandings of the fundamental theoretical bases of such conflicts might lead to more effective strategies for giving decision makers an understanding of the value of using IR results.

Emerging Views on the Character of Organizations

Predicting the evolution of organizational theory and its implications is a risky undertaking. One is apt to mistake contemporary fads for long-term conceptual shifts and, naturally, to assume that one's own notions are based on sound theory. Despite these hazards, this chapter examines several theoretical perspectives on organizational behavior that have some empirical support but that challenge the validity of some commonly held assumptions. It critiques several notions of organizational rationality: those that rely primarily on data and analysis in decision making, those that emphasize economic criteria when analyzing efficiency, those that assume organizations pursue goals, and those that use a problem-solving approach for dealing with organizational issues.

Some Common Views of Organizational Rationality

No attempt will be made to explore rationality broadly in this paper. A concise treatment of this topic by Friedland (1974) covers many of its facets. Friedland notes there is no simple definition of the term. Generally, *rationality* is seen as comprehending "the standards that ought to be used when decisions are made" (p. 2). Common assumptions about the nature of rational organizational behavior include the following:

• Organizations, or units within organizations, commonly are viewed as acting rationally when their decisions rely heavily on intelligence derived from research and analysis. When modern quantitative techniques for research and analysis are not given prominence, administrators' decision making behavior is often labeled irrational. Such labeling is particularly congenial to institutional researchers. After all, their major function is providing formal research and analysis to aid in decision making. Giving legitimacy to other sources of organizational intelligence risks the downgrading of their own importance.

• The effectiveness of decisions often is evaluated on the basis of economic standards of rationality. Institutional research staffs frequently have training in financial analysis. In addition, economic variables in organizations typically are more susceptible than noneconomic variables to quantification. Therefore institutional researchers frequently tend to emphasize economic efficiency and effectiveness as the rational basis for decision making.

• Organizational goals are commonly viewed as necessary to the making of rational decisions. When institutional administrators do not specify clear goals and develop plans to reach them, institutional researchers may question the rationality of their decision processes.

• Issues organizations confront are frequently conceived of as problems. These problems are viewed as having solutions. Once solutions are discovered, they are assumed to be applicable in similar situations. An effective, rational organization is one that discovers problems at an early stage and has the ability to design creative solutions. The data and analyses of institutional researchers help define problems and provide a basis for evaluating solutions.

Current organizational theories raise questions about the accuracy and utility of each of these assumptions as a rational way to view organizational behavior. Their limitations are described in the following sections.

Sources of Organizational Intelligence. Contemporary theories of organizational behavior suggest that there are a number of constraints on using data and analysis in decisions making and, additionally, that there are crucial nonquantitative sources of intelligence. Open systems theory (Katz and Kahn, 1978) views institutions as obtaining resources (*inputs*) that are transformed through some process into products or services (*outputs*). If an institution is to survive over time, its products or services must have sufficient value in the marketplace for it to exchange them for the resources it needs to maintain its production processes. This exchange of products and services for resources is accomplished through bargaining and salesmanship, which determine relative values and create markets. An *effective* institution provides products that are valued in the marketplace, and an *efficient* institution provides the largest amount of products from a given amount of resources (or a given amount of products from the least possible set of resources). The actors in such exchange cycles attempt to portray their products in the best possible light and to bargain for the most favorable exchange ratios.

Given this conception of organizational behavior, an educational institution may be viewed as importing a variety of resources such as students, faculty, legal authority, political support, organizational intelligence, and goods and services (or money to purchase goods and services) in exchange for some mix of educated citizens, research results, and public services. The information the institutions need to assess changes in the marketplace and in the performance of organizational processes comes from informal feedback from participants, according to cybernetic principles (Birnbaum, 1988), as they assess past actions, as well as from formal data gathering and analysis.

Contemporary views of proper organizational performance frequently place a major emphasis on data gathering and analysis as a means of gaining organizational intelligence and making wise decisions. The less structured, nonquantitative intelligence gained through feedback during exchange processes tends to be viewed as unscientific and irrational. Using informal feedback from past actions to take limited initiatives and then to make corrections based on consequences is seen as a wasteful process when analysis undertaken prior to implementing initiatives might reveal proper courses of action and justify bolder decisions. However, data are expensive, and many things are difficult to quantify. Frequently, there is little time for analysis, and predictions generally are uncertain. Consequently, much intelligence that organizations use comes from informally evaluating reactions to past courses of action and from a variety of informal sources such as newspapers, conferences, friends, and associates. Therefore, given the costs and limitations of formal data collection and analyses, an administrator should not be considered irrational when placing considerable weight on informal feedback from the marketplace.

This recognition that the information on which decisions rest comes from daily organizational interactions as well as from research and analysis should not be interpreted as downgrading the role of institutional research. It merely clarifies the environment in which valuable data gathering and analysis take place. A sensitivity to the various types and sources of information can give an institutional researcher a better appreciation of the broader intelligence administrators obtain from their daily interactions and from feedback regarding past actions. Institutional research may be viewed as supplementing but not supplanting other important sources of institutional intelligence.

Institutional administrators should share with institutional researchers the intelligence they get from other sources that is relevant to issues IR staff are addressing. Institutional research staff cannot be expected to be most helpful if they cannot construct their analyses in the context of the nonquantitative intelligence on issues possessed by senior policymakers.

Resources Involved in Organizational Exchange Processes. Frequently, economic variables and standards of rationality are emphasized when evaluating organizational decisions. Consequently, resources involved in organizational exchanges are often defined too narrowly. At least four classes of resources are exchanged in the organizational marketplace (Schmidtlein, 1977): *economic goods and services, social assets, human qualities and skills,* and *information.* The value placed on each resource when making decisions varies with circumstances. Frequently, a political resource or a cultural value outweighs an economic concern.

Economic Goods and Services. The first of these resources, economic goods and services, is the most common focus of policymaking. The rules of exchange for economic resources are more highly formulated than those for other resource exchanges. Economic data generally are more readily available for analysis than are data on other kinds of resources.

Social Assets. The second class of resources is social assets, such as status, legitimacy, authority, political power, association with core cultural values, and constituent trust. Theorists have given little attention to these assets as organization resources. Homans (1961), Blau (1964), and Ilchman and Uphoff (1969), among others, have developed some exchange theories of social resources. However, social resources are hard to measure and quantify so they are commonly neglected in many formal modes of policy analysis. Yet they are extremely important in perceptive administrators' calculations and typically are given significant, if not always explicit, weight in decision making.

Human Skills and Qualities. The third class of resources is composed of human skills and qualities. These resources also are difficult to analyze and quantify, but experienced administrators know their organizations are no better than the people they employ. Difficult choices are required when determining how much an outstanding person is worth to an organization in terms of salary, because a salary based on pure merit or on market demand for an occupation may raise equity concerns among other employees and any gain may be offset by the cost of lowered organizational morale. Sometimes a budget action based on economic considerations may cause the most competent persons to leave an organization, costing the organization more in overall terms than it realized from the budgetary savings. Also, purely financial decisions may have a negative affect on employee morale and result in lower productivity.

Information. The fourth class of resources is information. As is the case with social assets, people often fail to realize that information is exchanged and employed in ways designed to enhance the net advantages of persons and institutions. A common phenomenon is the bureaucrat who protects his position from ambitious subordinates by restricting their view of operations and discussions in progress. When individuals do not fully divulge information, there is a tendency to fault their rationality rather than to recognize that exchange process considerations also underlie their actions.

Implications of Differing Types of Resources. The decisions organizations make during exchange processes typically seek to maintain a balance among a total set of resources. A decision is irrational only if it does not balance various classes of resources in a way that betters the overall, long-range competitive position of the organization. Too narrow a focus on economic resources seldom produces the most satisfactory set of overall results. For example, a prestigious image is a very valuable asset to an institution of higher education. An institution's products are hard to measure and evaluate in the short run so popular perceptions of quality are particularly important. An institution receiving fewer student applications than it once did may see its interests better served by continuing to turn away less qualified students in order to maintain its reputation as a selective campus than by admitting less qualified students in order to increase its tuition revenues. The economic costs of the present tuition losses may be less crucial to the institution's long-term vitality than maintaining its academic reputation.

Institutional researchers must be sensitive to this full range of resources when engaged in research to support decision making. Their failure to do so no doubt is a frequent reason why policymakers sometimes ignore their analyses and recommendations. This broader view of resources may not only sensitize institutional researchers to factors that administrators themselves may be only dimly aware of, but it may also suggest new areas and approaches to research.

Utility of the Organizational Goal Concept. The conception of organizations as *goal seeking* is broadly accepted in much of the popular literature on management and undoubtedly shapes many institutional researchers' notions about management. Gross (1969) noted that "whatever else authors have to say on the general subject, there seems general agreement . . . that it is the dominating presence of a goal that marks off an 'organization' from all other kinds of systems" (p. 227).

This conception of organizations, however, is questioned by some scholars (Vickers, 1965). Georgiou (1973) produced one of the most thorough critiques of what he terms the "goal paradigm" and suggested a "counter paradigm" he believed better described organizational behavior. He observed that "rarely are analysts concerned with the question of whether organizations can be said to have goals; their existence is an unquestioned and unquestionable assumption. The only difficulty, insofar as any is recognized, lies in determining precisely what the goals of any particular organizations are" (p. 292). Georgiou's counter paradigm rests on viewing the individual as the basic strategic factor in organizations. An organization is conceived as composed of individuals and groups all striving to increase, maintain, or exchange the rewards (resources) they get from the organization in return for their contributions to it. The pursuit and the reconciliation of individual and group interests are the primary determinants of organizational behavior, not the pursuit of explicit or implicit organizational goals. Organizational decisions and courses of action are consequently based not on a priori goals but on perceptions of the implications of complex sets of exchange relationships and mutual accommodations among affected parties residing within and outside the organization. Parties to these transactions all possess power derived from a variety of sources and seek various outcomes. Therefore the power of top administrators and all others is delimited to varying degrees, depending on the issues and surrounding circumstances.

Vickers (1965) has suggested another way the notion of goals limits one's understanding of organizational decision making. He describes policymaking as "the setting of governing relations or norms, rather than in the more usual terms as the setting of goals, objectives or ends. The difference is not merely verbal; I regard it as fundamental. I believe that great confusion results from the common assumption that all course-holding can be reduced to the pursuit of an endless succession of goals" (p. 31).

A focus on goals, he believes, tends to downplay the importance of means. What organizational participants seek are changes in relationships, not particular goals with a particular individual values. In addition, he notes that organizations attempt to avoid threats as well as to achieve particular ends.

A useful analogy views an institution of higher education as a metal board dotted with moveable magnetic pegs, all connected in complex patterns with rubber bands of varying lengths and strengths. Each peg represents one role or variable. As each is shifted, tensions change among the other rubber bands, resulting in complex readjustments of their positions and achieving a new configuration, or equilibrium. A few bands connect pegs on the one board to pegs on adjoining boards, which represent external agencies and actors with which the institution has relationships. Thus shifts of pegs on any of several boards have reciprocal effects. Using another analogy, one could describe institutions as jigsaw puzzles. Altering the shape of one piece negatively affects its fit into the overall pattern of pieces. Given these models, one can visualize that changing one variable or group of variables in an organization has complex effects on other variables. Consequently, what one seeks in making organizational changes is a favorable set of new relationships among the variables (the pegs on the board or pieces of the puzzle).

These analogies illustrate how the notion of goals tends to obscure and oversimplify complex organizational relationships. Frequently, goals are stated in terms of the state of a few variables (the locations of one or a few pegs). Typically, little recognition is given to the effects that achieving narrowly defined goals might have on the full set of interconnected variables. Such a narrow focus on goals leads to suboptimizing behavior; maximizing one value at too great a cost to others. Thus the notion of goals can lead to oversimplified views about appropriate courses of action, resulting in serious unintended consequences.

Decision makers always seek to understand and anticipate the consequences of a course of action. However, because consequences generally are complex, and increasingly unpredictable after successive actions, there are limits to the utility of setting goals and employing a priori analyses as a basis for prescribing changes. These circumstances have given rise to the concept of *incrementalism,* set forth by Lindblom (1959), Wildavsky (1964), and others, as a strategy for making decisions. Incrementalism suggests that rather than engage in futile efforts to anticipate all significant changes that take place when adjustments occur in response to altering variables, rational administrators should act in limited, cautious ways and then assess reactions before proceeding further. This approach seems congruent with much behavior we observe in institutions.

An institutional researcher seeking clear statements of consistent, stable organizational goals will be disappointed in this environment. Participants can be expected to state their interests in ways that enhance their bargaining positions and maintain their flexibility to accommodate new intelligence on the various parties' positions and power relationships. They also will resist attempts to set goals that create suboptimizing behaviors and do not recognize the complex interactions among the variables involved in decisions. These circumstances no doubt explain why most institutional mission statements are general and nonspecific. Such statements must be able to win the support of important constituencies with divergent interests.

The Concept of Problems in Organizational Analysis. Unsatisfactory situations in institutions frequently are termed *problems*. An organizational problem often is viewed as analogous to a mathematical problem. A problem is assumed to have a best solution, and once discovered, this solution can be applied to similar problems in the future with similar results. However, taking a problem-solving perspective when seeking to improve organizational performance may misrepresent the actual nature of institutions and the character of their policy and decision processes.

The open systems view of organizations (that each organizations is composed of many parties, or subsystems, interacting to pursue their own interests and that these self-interests must be accommodated to the organization's collective interests) suggests that most decisions deal with reconciling conflicting values and perceptions. The substantive ends sought by various parties differ, and these differences must be resolved sufficiently to permit the collective enterprise to function. The resolution of value conflicts resulting from a particular decision generally does not alter the involved parties' underlying basic interests. It only temporarily subordinates some of their interests in order to preserve other, perhaps broader, interests. Basic interests remain and, as new opportunities arise, tend to reemerge periodically to reopen discussion. Thus conflicts, or problems, do not go away. They remain more or less submerged, awaiting a favorable opportunity to resurface. Over time, as changing conditions or perspectives give priority to various concerns, organizational attention shifts from one to another of these value conflicts or differences in perception. Cohen, March, and Olsen (1972) suggest the way in which many such organizational issues arise to gain attention is almost random. Debates in higher education over the balance between occupational and liberal education or the balance between teaching and research are examples of such regularly reopened conflicts.

One implication of this perspective that problems are never solved but only temporarily accommodated is that there are few if any general prescriptions for dealing with organizational issues that can be applied across a wide variety of settings. There may be some common approaches to conflict clarification and resolution. However, the actual solutions to specific conflicts in particular settings depend on complex interactions among the participants, all seeking their own interests. These interests, of course, include preserving the collective benefits provided by the organization, not just their more personal rewards.

This need to tailor decision processes to different environments and value orientations, or cultures, no doubt is another reason why universal prescriptions, such as PPBS, zero-based budgeting, and strategic planning have not achieved the success their proponents expected. These planning and budget decision processes represented an attempt to fit a variety of circumstances into a standard, and perhaps somewhat simplistic, decision process.

The slowness and politics that accompany decision making in higher education institutions, as a result of the factors described previously, are apt to frustrate an institutional researcher who views problems as technical questions that are solvable and that should not recur once solved. The accommodations made in reaching decisions and the balances sought in strategies employed to facilitate decisions all represent more or less fragile accords. These accords shift as the actors and conditions change over time. The institutional researcher provides resources in the form of data and analyses to the decision process. Only occasionally do these data and analyses point unambiguously toward an acceptable decision. Typically, data are only one ingredient in the discussion. Furthermore, many of the participants are likely to misunderstand the significance of the data and analyses or to misuse them for partisan advantage. Indeed, part of the dynamics of the interaction in decision situations is educating the participants about the value of data and analyses. However, unless institutional researchers accurately perceive the context in which the data are used, their efforts to make them relevant and to obtain recognition of their value are apt to be somewhat unsuccessful. Perhaps the term *issues* more accurately describes the actual nature of the circumstances higher education decision makers address. The word problem conveys an inaccurate sense of replicable and lasting solutions to human conflicts.

Conclusion

Institutional researchers, along with other administrators and faculty, frequently are perplexed by the behavior of institutional leaders. These officials frequently ignore data and analyses they receive and often do not support potentially useful data systems and studies. Sometimes they do not rely on available data when planning and budgeting. This behavior is sometimes blamed on a lack of a managerial competence, especially because many officials do not have professional management training. Yet many have considerable administrative experience. Consequently, their failure to use data and analysis more fully is also sometimes attributed to some type of human irrationality that afflicts organizations in general and, perhaps, institutions of higher education in particular. There is no doubt that in some circumstances officials act in ignorance and do not always act rationally. However, to some extent their decision making may also be explained by their differing conceptions of organizational behavior.

The emerging organizational theories described in this article suggest some limitations on the use of data and analysis in decision processes. These limitations have always been present though not always explicitly recognized. Explicit recognition of these limitations does not suggest a lesser role for institutional research. The capacity to accumulate and use data efficiently is increasing, and there is some evidence that the importance of data in decision making is increasing. However, new conceptions of organizational behavior clarify one's view of the role of data and analysis in decision making and especially the context in which they are used.

FRANK A. SCHMIDTLEIN is associate professor of higher education in the Department of Education Policy, Planning, and Administration at the University of Maryland, College Park.

7

Institutions of higher education are social organizations; learning theory is thus especially helpful in suggesting practical strategies for overcoming their organizational learning disabilities.

Teaching Institutional Research to the Learning-Inhibited Institution

Mark Bagshaw

Because of their values and knowledge structures, colleges and universities are frequently indisposed to make strategic choices based on institutional research. These organizations are *learning inhibited,* as a direct result of their dedication to producing, disseminating, and preserving knowledge. Consequently, institutional researchers who wish to be successful practitioners by influencing an institution's direction through their research must be skillful teachers as well. This chapter draws on individual and organizational learning theory to discuss how organizations learn, identifies and describes some of the more common learning disabilities that afflict institutions of higher education, and proposes some practical stratagems for their remedy.

How Does an Organization Learn?

The current state of organizational learning theory derives from developments in individual learning theory, where there has been a growing agreement over the years on the process by which learning takes place. In *The Process of Education,* a seminal work first published in 1960, Jerome Bruner (1963), characterized learning as involving

> three almost simultaneous processes. First, there is *acquisition* of new information—often information that runs counter to or is a replacement for what the person has previously known implicitly or explicitly. . . .

This chapter is based on a paper presented to the Northeast Association of Institutional Research, Providence, Rhode Island, Oct. 1988.

A second aspect of learning may be called *transformation*—the process of manipulating knowledge to make it fit new tasks. We learn to "unmask" or analyze information, to order it in a way that permits extrapolation or interpolation or conversions into another form. . . .

A third aspect of learning is *evaluation*—checking whether the way we have manipulated information is adequate to the task [p. 48].

Fourteen years later, in *Theory in Practice,* Argyris and Schön (1974) described a similar three-part learning process, arguing in a slightly later work that "human learning . . . need not be understood in terms of the 'reinforcement' or 'extinction' of patterns of behavior but as the *construction, testing, and restructuring* of a certain kind of knowledge" (Argyris and Schön, 1978, p. 10; emphasis added). More recent descriptions of the learning process do not differ substantially. Lord and Foti (1986), for example, describe a learning process that consists of *gathering information* and *integrating* this information with a "highly *structured,* preexisting *knowledge system*" in order to *interpret* the world and *generate "appropriate behaviors"* (p. 20; emphasis added).

If these later conceptualizations of the learning process display an evolutionary development, it is in incorporating the realization that knowledge—whether derived from observation of the physical or the social world—has implications that shape the individual's behavior. Like Lord and Foti, a number of contemporary learning theorists follow Bartlett (1932) in conceiving of these action implications of an individual's knowledge system as *schemata*—hypothetical mental structures that predispose an individual to particular ways of viewing phenomena, integrating new information with his or her knowledge system, retrieving it from memory, and using it as the basis for action: "In essence, a schema provides observers with a knowledge base that serves as a guide for the interpretation of information, action, and expectations" (Lord and Foti, 1986, p. 22; see also Graesser, Woll, Kowalski, and Smith, 1980; Taylor and Crocker, 1981).

Organizational learning theory, although covering a different domain from individual learning, has developed by focusing on related problems with similar ideas. The critical linking concept between individual and organizational learning is *organizational social cognition:* organizations are social entities created by individuals who, through their interactions, create the shared learning structure of an organization. The definitive formulation is Karl Weick's, described here by Dennis Gioia (1986): "Weick (1979) argues that it is not only behaviors that become structured in organizations but also information and shared meaning—meaning that has been socially constructed, negotiated, and consensually validated. . . . Through the development and structuring of shared meaning and understanding, cycles of interlocked behavior become sensible. The storehouse of knowledge about 'cycles of interlocked behavior' are the individual and consensual scripts held by organization members" (p. 62).

A good illustration of the congruity theorized to exist between the individual and the organization in the learning process appears in an article written by the head of planning for the Royal Dutch/Shell group of companies (de Geus, 1988). He asks the question, "How does a company learn and adapt?" and he describes a sequential learning process that consists of company executives' *absorbing* new data or developing new ways of looking at existing data, *incorporating* these new data as new information into their mental models of business, *drawing conclusions* from the revised mental models, *testing* these conclusions against experience, and *acting* on the basis of the altered model (pp. 70–71).

Table 7.1 attempts to model, in a heuristic framework, the learning process as described by the researchers I have cited here. Implicit in the attempt to move beyond the individual organizational participant is *a recognition of the fundamentally social character of organizational learning as distinguished from individual learning*. Organizational learning results from *shared* assumptions, beliefs, and values—and shared structures for realizing them. As noted by Argyris and Schön (1978), "Organizational learning is not merely individual learning, yet organizations learn only through the experiences and actions of individuals" (p. 9).

Impediments to Organizational Learning

Whether we advise presidents, provosts, deans, department heads, or faculty committees, most of us can provide anecdotal evidence about the difficulty of attempting to modify existing knowledge structures in colleges and universities, and there are a number of reasons why this type of organization is likely to be more learning inhibited than some others.

Effects of Institutionalization. Colleges and universities are *institutions* of higher education: that is, they are social institutions. One of their chief responsibilities is to preserve and disseminate societal values—the knowledge and the attitudes toward knowledge that the culture deems valuable. Some thirty years ago, Philip Selznick (1957) captured the value-centered distinction between institution and organization: "'to institutionalize' is to *infuse with value* beyond the technical requirements of the task at hand. The prizing of social machinery beyond its technical role is largely a reflection of the unique way in which it fulfills personal or group needs. Whenever individuals become attached to an organization or a way of doing things as persons rather than technicians, the result is a prizing of the device for its own sake" (p. 17).

Unfortunately, the same characteristics that enable an institution to preserve and transmit societal values make that institution risk averse and inimical to change. New learning is a fundamental form of organizational change. As a result, who has greater potential to change (and threaten) the very identity of an institution than the person whose avowed preoccupation is institutional research?

Table 7.1. A Framework for the Learning Process

Bruner (1963) (Individual as Unit of Analysis)	Argyris and Schön (1974) (Individual or Organization as Unit of Analysis)	Lord and Foti (1986) (Individual or Organization as Unit of Analysis)	de Geus (1988) (Dominant Coalition as Unit of Analysis)	Emerging Organizational Learning Model (Collectivity of Individuals Interacting Organizationally as Unit of Analysis)
Acquisition of information		Information gathering	Absorption	Observation and intuition
Analysis of information	Construction of knowledge	Integration with knowledge system	Incorporation in executives' mental models	Search for meaning congruence
Transformation (manipulating knowledge to fit new tasks)		Interpretation of the world	Drawing conclusions	Generating inferences, hypotheses
Evaluation	Testing of knowledge		Testing conclusions	Social testing; *consensual validation*
	Restructuring of knowledge		(Alteration of executives mental models)	Mutual adjustment of individual intuition and organizational knowledge system
		Exhibition of appropriate behavior	Concerted executive action (decision making)	Change in predispositions for action, intuition

Teachers' Need to Become Learners. A second source of inhibition derives from the specific technical functions performed by colleges and universities, namely, teaching and research. Teachers and researchers frequently are disabled by their own learning: if learning consists of the transfer and integration of learning structures, rather than "simply the mastery of facts and techniques" (Bruner, 1963, p. 12), then the intrusion of institutional research with new, alternative, and often *alien* (outside the social sciences) knowledge structures and unfamiliar ways of viewing presents, minimally, the need to incorporate or synthesize this information and, maximally, the need to *deconstruct* one's existing knowledge structure in order to reassemble around a new structural principle that substantially revises one's knowledge base. This revised knowledge base may have radically different implications for individual and for institutional action. A similar process has been posited by Kuhn (1970) in describing at length the process of scientific paradigm replacement in the sciences.

Lack of Legitimacy. A distinct learning impediment is that members of the collegium perceive institutional researchers as lacking legitimacy. It is not so much that institutional researchers are singled out for malignant neglect—some arts and sciences faculty view professional colleagues in business and education with the same contempt—as that some faculty (presidents, provosts, and so on) start from a mental model or knowledge structure that finds institutional research activities unrecognizable or—as when researchers lend themselves to such crass exercises as seeking to predict or increase the size of the entering freshman class—beneath notice.

Dispersion of Governing Authority. In most organizations there are relatively clear lines of authority for making decisions that permit organizational action. Social interaction is needed for organizational learning to take place, but what has passed for organizational learning and action in most large and complex business organizations is limited to a centralized leadership cadre (that is, managers and owners). In de Geus's example (1988), once the Royal Dutch/Shell executives had been mutually informed and had altered their mental models, organizational action was understood to be a matter of course. In institutions of higher education, however, it is less simple to identify the appropriate decision makers because decision-making authority for *most* decisions is dispersed across and up and down the organization. Faculty typically have a substantial voice in matters of curriculum development, faculty promotion and tenure, and student admission and evaluation criteria, as well as substantial influence on resource allocation and other conditions of employment. As a result the watchword for presidents, provosts, deans, and department heads in decision making on matters of any substance is always *adequate consultation*. In this governance framework a well-defined concept, a critical need, a strategic opportunity can be diffused and go unmet and unavailed, and the implications for organizational action buried.

Suspicion of Dehumanizing Quantification. The rudimentary quantitative instruments of the institutional researcher are subject to suspicion in some quarters of the academy. This suspicion typically comes to a head over measurements of human performance that imply movement or reallocation of funds, positions, or personnel—particularly as these may affect the teaching and research functions. Quantitatively oriented student outcome measures, teaching effectiveness quotients, quantitative research productivity profiles, faculty flow models—*all* have generated hostility, resistance, and monkey-wrenching at one time or another.

Given the ambiguity of the technical functions of teaching and research, and the bias toward the personal, the idiosyncratic, and the autonomous of many who perform those functions, it is not surprising that any sign of insensitivity to the essentially humane nature of much of the academic enterprise should provoke characterizations of institutional researchers as "soulless quants" who, when they seek to focus on the central mysteries, miss the point of the exercise. Obviously, this characterization is just as reductive as the assumption that those who challenge the indiscriminate application of complex measures are uninformed romantics. The point here is that such prejudicial characterizations and suspicions can prevent institutions from learning how to use institutional research effectively.

Global Displacement of Expertise. One of the greatest impediments to incorporating the insights of institutional research in the organizational knowledge system is a variation on the age-old theme of Ignorance Militant: presidents, provosts, deans, you, and I have been conditioned to acquiesce all too readily in the unexamined assumption that a faculty member's specific disciplinary expertise qualifies him or her as general expert on all institutional issues and problems. Of course, no one believes in the validity of this global application of specific expertise more unexaminedly than the faculty member who has used it to solve all the institution's problems.

Unfocused Presentations and Uncertain Rewards. For academics— including presidents, provosts, deans, and department heads—the rewards of focusing their limited decision-making attention time on institutional research issues are uncertain. Consequently, attending to institutional research may not have much appeal for many persons in the academy. For institutional researchers, this argues for making the best use of any presentation opportunities. On the one hand, a recurring example of poor use of an opportunity is the researcher who entertains academic decision makers with long asides on the glories of technical minutiae. Maybe some presidents are keen to kick back on kurtosis, but I don't know one. On the other hand is the researcher who, perhaps in order not to appear to be presuming beyond his or her station, presents the institutional leadership with the data but without a sense of their potential impact on the institution and without a feel for their implications for institutional action.

Remedial and Evasive Action

If the learning of colleges and universities is impeded by attitudes and values that buoy up and perpetuate defective organizational learning structures, how can institutional researchers get their messages across?

Plant Structure. The most useful starting point is to plant structuring devices that will help faculty and administrators to understand what institutional researchers think they are doing. One basic way of planting these devices is to familiarize your institution with the institutional research process whereby, as a result of observation and measurement, an institutional researcher transforms phenomena into *data,* interprets these data and creates *information,* and in exercising judgment about the meaning of this information for the institution, adds to the institution's possibilities for *knowledge* about itself (Cleveland, 1985, pp. 21–23; Johnson and Christal, 1985, p. 5). The usefulness of this approach is that it replicates what many academic researchers do in their own work (and it resembles the emerging learning theory model, outlined in Table 7.1). As de Geus (1988) points out, planners and researchers sometimes start out with a mental model that is unrecognizable to those they are trying to educate. To connect new information with some familiar aspect of academics' existing knowledge structure is just good pedagogy.

Of course, knowledge for its own sake is not a sufficient end for the institutional researcher, and so a necessary second step in the structure planting process is to make apparent the links between, on the one hand, possibilities for knowledge gained from institutional research and, on the other hand, the resolution of institutional problems and the realization of institutional values, mission, and goals: for example, What should we be doing to serve the area's adult learners? What's the regional market for new doctorally qualified English professors? Has the math aptitude of our freshman admits improved over the past ten years? How does our ten year experience compare with that of those institutions with whom we share the greatest number of applicants? Just how vulnerable *is* the educational mission of this institution under a scenario of no mandatory faculty retirement at age seventy?

Institutional research will be valued and attended to by other institutional participants to the extent that it can be shown to help them generate answers to questions that have meaning and relevance for them, to the extent that suggestive answers from institutional research account more satisfactorily for troubling phenomena than other answers provided from participants' existing knowledge structure, and to the extent that participants can be enticed to enlarge their knowledge to consider questions that they have not formulated before.

Capture the Flag. From the viewpoint of institutional survival and prosperity, there is no higher calling than conducting institutional research. If your institutional leadership doesn't know it, and show it, you have a major public relations problem. What you will need to do in order to start to turn the situation around is to capture the ear of the most powerful source of legitimate authority on your reporting line. You begin to do this in three ways: (1) always give full measure, pressed down; (2) never go around your immediate supervisor (although talking loudly over his or her shoulder is permitted); and (3) always give clear indications—in a written memorandum with an appropriately targeted circulation—when your data show significant implications for institutional action at a high level. (The memo is like blood in the water: it *guarantees* the big fish will find you!) As a result of these actions, you now have the attention and goodwill of someone like your president or provost. This person is the best solution to any legitimacy problems you have with the rest of the institution, and, with a few well-reasoned words from you, will serve willingly as the institutional research office's public relations flak. Furthermore, because people who play with giants sometimes get crushed, this person will protect you from chaired professors run amok and other loose cannons. Why this person does this is that he or she knows the information you provide is crucial to the institution, and believes that you are good at what you do. The reason he or she believes this is that you constantly reinforce the belief by providing additional evidence.

Disperse Ownership. The dispersion of governing authority across the institution is a major impediment to organizational learning and organizational action. One remedial action is to strategically disperse ownership of the institutional research office across the institution. Anatol Rapoport (1972) points out that one of the reasons parables are so memorable is that they permit their hearers to participate in the mystery of unfolding their meaning. In much the same way, institutional researchers will get their message across to the extent they provide opportunities for faculty and administrators to build institutional research into their knowledge systems and predispositions for action on behalf of the institution. The operative term is *strategic:* obviously, not all institutional information can be freely disseminated to every institutional participant and department, and not all institutional participants and departments are interested in the same information; however, where there is a match, an opportunity is created for the cultivation of ownership—by exploring interests, supplying meaningful informational reports, and scanning the environment and alerting participants and departments to significant changes. This strategy is based on the creation of a "personalized" office of institutional research and the subsequent exploitation of a number of discrete market segments.

Exercise Discrimination. Professional peer judgment—such as faculty evaluation of colleagues for tenure and promotion—is at the heart of the academic enterprise and central to what it means to be a faculty member. The process is inherently subjective, and the addition of reliable quantitative measures that assist in these judgments is welcomed by most faculty. However, measures that seem to supplant this subjective judgment—for example, by substituting a teaching performance score, in the name of objectivity—often are seen as suspect by faculty, as are the individuals who create such measures and argue for their use. The easiest way to convince faculty that institutional researchers are not evil scientists who debase their calling to curry favor with administrators and pander to legislatures is to show a little judiciousness in the application of quantitative measures. It is important to convince faculty of this, because despite short-term appearances it is not legislatures, boards of governors, and administrators who determine the strategic direction of an institution; in the long haul it is the will of the faculty. Institutional researchers lose neither face nor influence by public expressions of concern that their instruments be applied appropriately in the arenas of faculty evaluation, student assessment, and institutional policymaking.

Trade Shadow for Substance. Anthropologists tell us that among members of the tribe of academe the word for bona fide members of the tribe is the same as the word for human being: that word is *faculty*. (It is said that the literal, root meaning of the phrase *tenured faculty member* is "he-who-walks-totally-erect-and-is-the-glory-of-the-universe.") My own observation suggests that if faculty want to represent themselves as masters of the university, there are few rewards for institutional researchers who oppose them. With regard to the specific problem created by the tendency to globalize expertise, the solution is to insist that faculty bring to the party their legitimate strengths—the same analytical skills, reflectiveness, and objectivity that they bring in their better moments to teaching and research, as well as their particular disciplinary learning model and personal experience of the institution, all of which provide at once a unique perspective on the issues in question and, in the aggregate, suggestive directions for future research. To paraphrase Socrates and former Secretary of Education William Bennett, if the unexamined life is not worth living, the unexamined faculty pronouncement is not worth hearing. I know few academics so arrogant as to hold out against that logic.

Think Strategically. All of this discussion argues for a *proactive,* shaping role in the institution for the practitioners of institutional research: a role that involves defining problems and opportunities; underlining their relevance; pointing out the concatenations, interrelationships, and interaction effects; talking about the consequences; and selling the benefits. The operative mode for this role is facilitative: successful teaching, after all, is less lecture and inspired revelation than it is providing opportunities in which discovery and learning can take place. In operation the technique is not so much to impose structure as to plant it and husband its growth.

Institutional researchers also need to master the art of distinguishing a learning opportunity. As a rule of thumb, changing circumstances are a golden opportunity for educating members of the organization whose lives will be affected by the change. Obviously, there is considerable room for individual receptivity and ability here: not every president is comfortable receiving action recommendations from the institutional research office—even when the existing knowledge base clearly is inadequate—but many, many presidents don't know what they want till they see what they can get. Presidents, provosts, and deans—like other people—give their attention primarily to those things that have meaning for them, and it is all too easy for an undereducated institutional leader to dismiss an array of admissions data with thanks and an admonition to staff that "we must all remain truly mindful of the importance of good student enrollments to accomplishing institutional goals."

Conclusion

To counteract the tendency for the institutional research office to be perceived primarily as the indefatigable source of a succession of Gibbonesque "damned, thick, square" and perfunctory maintenance reports—and that is indeed the default setting for expectations at many institutions—institutional researchers have to set the frame and shape the intellectual expectations of the leadership. You don't have to hit 'em with a board, but you owe it to your profession and your self-esteem to teach them not to bring garbage *in* to your interactions, and you do that by structuring, stretching, and then rewarding their expectations.

MARK BAGSHAW is associate professor of management and leadership, Marietta College, Marietta, Ohio.

8

As a postsecondary knowledge industry emerges and institutions consider redesigning themselves, institutional researchers need to become knowledge industry analysts.

The Role of Institutional Research: From Improvement to Redesign

Marvin W. Peterson

Any discussion of the historical evolution and future direction of institutional research inevitably reflects the unique perspective each author brings to the task. The authors of the previous chapters have each provided theirs. In this chapter, I incorporate three perspectives: professional self-reflection, institutional adaptation, and higher education as an industry.

First, *professional self-reflection,* examining the role and function of institutional research (IR), has been a major preoccupation of this field ever since the first national forum in 1961. What is IR? What is its institutional role? How is it defined? What are its primary functions and activities? How is it organized? What skills and expertise does it require? Is it a profession? These have all been the focus of continual debate in our forums, our workshops, and our publications. Our literature reflects the endless debate over the nature and role of institutional research. The role has been variously described as a management service function (Brumbaugh, 1960), an autonomous institutional critic (Dressel, 1971), an institutional or an organizational intelligence officer (Tetlow, 1984), a change agent and action researcher (Lindquist, 1981), an institutional advocate or political partisan (Firnberg and Lasher, 1983), a telematics technologist (Bernard Sheehan, cited in Peterson and Corcoran, 1985), a management and decision support function, (Saupe, 1990), a policy analyst (Gill and Saunders, 1992; Terenzini, 1993), and many other variations. How institutional research has evolved as a profession (Peterson and Corcoran, 1985), whether it is "art or science" (Fincher, 1985), how professional development for the field occurs (Cope, 1979), and what its ethics and standards are or should be (Schiltz, 1992) have been examined and discussed.

This practice of professional self-reflection has served us well as a professional field, as an association, and as individual professionals. It is my hope that this volume and this chapter will aid our understanding of our past and future.

Second, the Association for Institutional Research (AIR) officially defines institutional research as "research leading to improved understanding, planning and operating of institutions of postsecondary education." But in my view, institutional research has been more than a servant of institutional improvement and management. From my perspective, institutional research has flourished as an institutional function and a profession because it has contributed to institutions' *adaptive function* and has played a major role in fostering and assisting institutional change. As I look back briefly on the development and contribution of the field, institutional research may best be understood by examining how we tackled the major issues facing our institutions and helped our institutions accommodate to them. We can best understand the changing role and contribution of institutional research by examining the interface between an institution and its environment and how institutions adapt to challenges at that interface. This chapter suggests that the major challenge facing institutional research may be more daunting in the years ahead—to assist our institutions to address changing conditions that require not just organizational improvement but institutional redesign and transformation.

And finally, in looking ahead this chapter takes an *industry* perspective. Although this term may be as threatening to some college administrators today as *management* was twenty-five years ago, it offers a useful analytical perspective that gives us insight into today's institutional challenges.

Adopting these three perspectives, this chapter reviews briefly the evolving role and contribution of institutional research to institutional adaptation, summarizes how societal conditions are reshaping the postsecondary industry, and suggests some implications for institutional research as institutions respond to the emerging postsecondary knowledge industry. Each of these three topics is illustrated by a table.

A Brief History of the Evolution of Institutional Research

Although there were institutional research studies prior to World War II, the development of institutional research as an administrative process or function is primarily a post-1950s development, so our analytical interpretation begins there (see Table 8.1). As external conditions affecting higher, or postsecondary, education have changed over the past forty years, the primary press on institutional management, the view of institutions as organizations, and the primary focus of institutional performance have shifted. Institutional research developed concurrently, helped institutions adapt to meet these challenges, and has been shaped by the same forces.

Table 8.1. The Evolution of Institutional Research: Adapting to Institutional Challenges

	External Conditions	Management Press	Organization and Governance	Performance Focus	Primary Role of IR
1950					
	Growth and expansion	Direction and accountability	Formal and collegial	Resources	Descriptive, developmental
1960					
	Disruption and demands	Order, control, and access	Political and open systems	Reputation	Analytical, comparative
1970					
	Economic recession	Efficiency and market orientation	Managerial and market	Results Productivity and efficiency	Evaluative, quantitative
1980					
	Constraint and quality	Reduction Reallocation and retrenchment Effectiveness and quality	Organized anarchy Cultural and conglomerate	Results: Goal achievement Student performance Structure and reengineer	Analytical, comparative Planning and policy analysis
1990					
2000	Educational challenges and new constituents	Redesigning institutions	Entrepreneurial networks Alliances and joint ventures Virtual organizations	Redefine industry and university role Redirect mission and relationships Reorganize process and structure Reform workplace culture	Knowledge industry analyst Anticipatory, proactive

1950s and 1960s Growth and Expansion. Following World War II and continuing through the 1960s, U.S. higher education experienced an unprecedented period of growth and expansion, which reflected strong public support, expanding enrollment demands, and increasing government financial support. During this period the pressure on institutional management was to provide a sense of direction for the growing institution and to account for the extensive human, financial, and physical resources it was absorbing in order to justify that support.

Two internally oriented models of organization emerged at this time to help administrators understand and manage growing institutions. First was the notion of a formal rational or bureaucratic organization (Stroup, 1966), which focused on building rational structures to administer and mechanisms to account for growing resource flows and needs. The second was the collegial model, which viewed postsecondary institutions as communities of learners (Goodman, 1964), professionals (Clark, 1971), or constituents with a common community of interests (Millett, 1962). Both models reflected notions of colleges and universities as self-contained educational organizations.

Institutional performance during this era focused primarily on accounting for resources. With encouragement from the American Council on Education (ACE), the Western Interstate Commission for Higher Education, the New England Board of Higher Education, and the Southern Regional Education Board, workshops on institutional research were held that spawned the formal development of our emerging field (Doi, cited in Cope, 1979). The focus was on developing means of accounting for resources and on conducting studies of student characteristics; faculty work and activities; admissions, enrollment, and placement; space utilization; and income and expenses. These studies were basic, descriptive data crunching by current standards. During the 1960s, issues of institutional size and complexity and concerns about standards also gave rise to more complex institutional self-studies and increasingly data-driven accreditation reviews.

The first institutional researchers forum, in 1961, was convened by invitation. A second forum was opened to broader participation the following year, in response to institutional interests. The rapidly growing interest in expansion led to the founding of AIR in 1964 (Doi, cited in Cope, 1979). Most of the early institutional research directors reported to the institution's president. Clearly institutional research was contributing to managing growth and expansion. Rourke and Brooks' *The Managerial Revolution in Higher Education* (1966) summarized this expanding era and described the development of institutional research as a critical management function.

Disruption and Demands. As outlined in Table 8.1, higher education's bubble burst in the late 1960s and early 1970s. Disruptions emanated from both inside and outside the university. Students were dissatisfied with the increasingly large, impersonal, and formally structured institutions and with increasingly professionalized faculty with scholarly rather than teaching interests. Societal issues such as the U.S. role in the Vietnam War, the civil rights movement, and the free speech movement found fertile ground among liberal and disaffected faculty and students, who wanted a forum to express their views. The pressure on institutional management was to keep order or control on campus and to ensure greater access for minority and less traditional students.

Reflecting the general organizational literature (Katz and Kahn, 1978), models of colleges and universities as organizations began to recognize them as open systems. More important, they were viewed as political organizations (Baldridge, 1971) made up of competing constituencies. This era also coincided with the growth of state systems, which brought public institutions increasingly under political scrutiny (Berdahl, 1971) and added a new layer of complexity to institutional governance and external reporting.

Interestingly, as the emergent, internal political governance model attempted to incorporate and mollify the conflicting constituents, the external emphasis on performance shifted to enhancing the external reputation of higher education, Indeed, the first reputational studies of higher education were sponsored by the American Council on Education (Cartter, 1966; Roose and Anderson, 1970) and focused primarily on graduate research universities. This emphasis on reputational quality determined by peer judgment later expanded to most institutional types and many professional or disciplinary segments. Of course today colleges and universities have reputational ratings done by magazines and noneducational organizations and based on the judgment of their business and consumer customers. At the state level, interest in financial cost issues, program review, and institutional duplication intensified. An institution's political reputation demanded more detailed accounting and reporting for all resources.

Although institutional researchers did not start reputational studies nor create the state pressures, they responded. They became more analytical and comparative in their approach rather than relying on descriptive reports. They were eager to examine the correlates of quality programming, deepened their interest in studies of student behavior, strengthened their resource reporting capacity, and become aware of the potential uses, value, and abuses of such studies.

Recession and Constraint. From the mid-1970s to the early 1980s, an economic recession and the realization that the end of the postwar baby boom would dampen enrollment growth forced a new reality on many campuses. State, federal, and other external agencies were also responding to their own resource constraints. They demanded greater institutional accountability for resources and were becoming more sophisticated in collecting and analyzing data and in asking tough management questions. At the same time, the 1972 Higher Education Amendments shifted federal student aid distribution from institutions directly to the student, and federal agencies and legislation began using the term *postsecondary education*. This vastly increased the number of institutions and students eligible for student aid. These changes pressed institutional management to focus on improving internal efficiency and to seek new markets for students.

New organizational models now began to emphasize colleges and universities either as managerial models built on comprehensive information systems that used resource simulation models to inform decisions (Lawrence and Service, 1977) or as market-oriented models (Kotler, 1975) designed to identify and attract new students.

This new reality led to a new emphasis on performance based on results—not just on inputs or resources used. Initially, this focus encouraged quantitative measures of productivity (output measures of numbers of graduates, degrees granted, and so forth) or efficiency (indices of cost per degree or per course, faculty workload, faculty specialization, and so forth). Cameron Fincher (1985) has chronicled the increased use of evaluative research approaches as institutional researchers developed and implemented management information systems and added management by objective (MBO) studies, demographic forecasting, program planning and budgeting systems (PPBS) and zero-based budgeting, cost studies, resource utilization studies, and even economic benefit analysis to their repertoire during this period.

Enrollment and Financial Constraints. By the mid-1980s, it became apparent that improved management, marketing, and efficiency would not be sufficient. Economic constraints continued, and new demands for public funds grew. Demographic characteristics suggested real declines in traditional-aged students and likely changes in their economic, ethnic, and educational background. Competition increased as proprietary institutions and other organizations vied with more traditional higher education institutions for students and funds. The management press was to reduce, reallocate, and retrench (Mortimer and Tierney, 1979), to carefully examine programs and to focus on more limited purposes, and to become more effective not just efficient.

Colleges and universities were now being viewed not just as more open institutions that responded to their environments. They were now strategic organizations (Keller, 1983; Peterson, 1980), which could revise purposes and priorities, change clientele and program mixes, and seek a strategic market niche in the higher education industry. Other new organizational models viewed them as flexible, decentralized conglomerates, as matrix organizations (Alpert, 1986), as organized anarchies (Cohen and March, 1974), and as unique cultural entities (Tierney, 1990).

The latter part of the 1980s and early 1990s has brought a curious twist to this era of constraints. Criticism of U.S. education, first at the K–12 level (National Commission on Excellence in Education, 1983) and then at the higher education level (Study Group on Conditions of Excellence in American Higher Education, 1984), led some academic leaders and many public policy officials to challenge colleges and universities to measure performance results in terms of educational and instructional quality and of student learning outcomes and to encourage the use of student and academic assessment in a variety of modes and purposes. The quality improvement movement, popular in U.S. business and industry as a way to recapture economic supremacy, added another dimension to performance assessment, focusing on total institutional functioning.

Once again institutional researchers were in the foray. Strategic planning studies and mission reviews; marketing, recruitment, and need and demand studies; student, faculty, and program evaluation and assessment; studies of utilization and condition of capital facilities; design of decision support systems; administrative staff studies; and policy analysis were all added to the IR arsenal (Fincher, 1985). Most recently, the elusive performance indicators have been a focus of attention. In expanding these efforts, institutional researchers have also come to rely more on qualitative approaches.

Implications. The history just outlined contains several useful themes as we enter the twenty-first century. First, the major challenges that have shaped institutional management, organizational models, and performance criteria were primarily external. Second, those challenges reflect an environment that has become more complex, less munificent, and more critical or threatening. Third, the challenges have been dealt with primarily by managerial responses in institutional governance, management, and performance patterns. Although program offerings have been modified and student demographics have changed, the basic teaching and learning processes and academic functions have been affected very little. Fourth, institutional research has played a critical role in helping institutions respond to the challenges and in the process has expanded its role and array of activities (although this is often accomplished through a dispersed set of institutional offices and activities rather than through a central institutional research office). And finally, the new models or patterns, including our institutional research activities, do not supersede the earlier ones. Rather, understanding institutional research can be seen as part of a more complex understanding of the organizational, management, and performance patterns in postsecondary institutions. These contextual insights are helpful as we look to the future.

Challenges of the Twenty-First Century

As suggested by the outline in Table 8.1, the decade ahead will pose serious challenges, both for postsecondary institutions and for institutional researchers, that are quite different from those of our past four decades. In discussing these challenges I side neither with Peter Drucker (1995), who speculates that universities as we now know them will cease to exist in twenty years, nor with the traditional view that colleges and universities, only slightly modified, will always exist. A more fundamental change than postsecondary institutions have ever faced in the past lies ahead—a *redefinition* of the industry that could lead to institutional *redesign*.

An Industry Perspective. Industry reflects a "set of related organizations which utilize similar resources, attract similar clients, and produce similar services." Clearly, postsecondary education is a definable segment of the educational industry. Porter (1980), in his study of forces reshaping competition in an industry, posits four key forces: the bargaining power of customers (students), the bargaining power of suppliers, the threat of new organizational entrants, and the threat of substitute services. I suggest that two other forces are also critical—intensity of competition and innovation in the core technology of the industry.

Viewed as an industry, higher education has undergone two transitions over the past fifty years: from an industry of traditional higher education to one of mass higher education and from an industry of mass higher education to one of postsecondary education. These transitions occurred primarily as a result of only two of the six forces: the addition of new organizations (community colleges and proprietary institutions) to the competitive mix and the new bargaining power of consumers as their numbers increased and the control of financial aid shifted to them. But after both transitions, colleges and universities are still competing with other institutions, and they have only minimally modified the process of delivering education.

As we enter the twenty-first century, the rapid technological changes affecting education receive much attention, but my argument is that at least six societal conditions and six industry reshaping forces are interacting to promote change. (A seventh condition, resource constraint, both affects how institutions respond and enhances competition. Because it is a condition we all clearly understand, it is not discussed here.)

We understand the impact of these six conditions on institutions individually, thus it is the collective impact on the industry that is outlined in Table 8.2 and summarized here.

Changing Patterns of Diversity. The challenge of dealing with cultural diversity and its concomitant educational and economic deprivation is widely recognized as a social reality, a public policy issue, and an institutional reality. Colleges and universities have had some success in improving access to postsecondary education for various disadvantaged groups, but their record of successful retention and graduation is still inadequate in many fields and at the graduate level (Carter and Wilson, 1993; Musil and others, 1995).

There are several lessons from experience and from the trends. First, the operant definition of cultural diversity is constantly changing. The concern, initially for African American minorities in the 1960s, has expanded to include numerous other racially underrepresented groups. Issues of gender, sexual preference, and economic or educational disadvantage have further expanded and fragmented the focus of diversity efforts. Second, the numbers of almost all of minority groups are increasing and will continue to do so for the foreseeable future. Third, members of most minority groups have become well organized and are becoming more effective political voices both on campuses and in the public policy arena. Fourth, the public policy and institutional response strategy has shifted—from separate but equal, to nondiscrimination, to preferences, to affirmative action, to multicultural emphasis. The current debates about and attempts to dismantle affirmative action are likely to be heated and to continue. But the impacts on the forces reshaping the industry are more revealing.

The number of both the individuals and the categories defined as educationally disadvantaged continues to grow (see Table 8.2). As potential learning customers influencing public policy, the minority political caucus groups at the institutional, state, and national level are growing and becoming a more powerful force influencing institutional resource suppliers.

Although few new minority postsecondary institutions have been founded in recent decades, the number of existing institutions becoming de facto minority institutions is increasing rapidly (approximately one in five postsecondary institutions now has an enrollment in which ethnic minority students exceed 50 percent of the student body). Several new minority-oriented professional associations have been founded to serve these institutions and to represent their constituents' interests. The increase of

Table 8.2. Challenges and Forces Reshaping the Postsecondary Industry

Six Societal Conditions or Challenges	Six Forces That Reshape					
	Bargaining Power of Customers	Bargaining Power of Suppliers	Threat of New Organizational Entrants	Threat of Substitute Services	Innovations in Core Technology	Intensity of Competition
Diversity	More defined groups Increasing numbers	More and stronger political groups	Minority institutions and associations	New programs and services	New academic and research perspectives	Among students and among institutions
Telematics revolution	More access and numbers Individualized needs	Telematics firms control key educational resources	Telecommunications, computing, and information firms	Training firms and merged entertainment and telecommunications	New interactive, individualized teaching, learning, and research	New cross-industry competition
Quality reform	Increased focus on learner needs	Increased attention to client demands		Minor new training options	New mode of management Limited use by academics	Improvements in efficiency and effectiveness
Economic productivity	Increased career-oriented pressure	Government and industry needs	New role or interorganizational patterns	Many new groups and governmental agencies	May redirect teaching and research	New regional, state, or national agencies
Postsecondary relearning	New groups of postsecondary learners	Employer-based funding sources	Many new forms emerging	Corporate and governmental education programs	Emphasis on personalized content and delivery	Ill-defined market Potential of many sources
Globalization	Not clearly defined Highly specialized	Nations and institutions	Currently informal or limited arrangements	Emergent use of technology	Traditional or new technology	Yet to be determined

minority-oriented academic and support programs has often been seen as adding substitute services. Although not directly affecting the core technology of postsecondary education, the advent of minority programs and of new faculty staffing patterns, student and faculty interaction patterns, and academic perspectives and research agendas has influenced the processes of teaching and research in significant ways. Clearly, pressure to enhance diversity affects all six forces and has created intense competition among institutions attempting to attract increased numbers of more diverse students, faculty, and staff.

The Telematics Revolution. Probably the most pervasive challenge to the postsecondary industry and its institutions is the rapid expansion of interactive telecommunications networks linking student and faculty to extensive data resources via workstations capable of presenting information by integrating text, audio, and video. This technology is expanding rapidly in areas such as distance and continuing education to serve older students but also is serving more traditional students. Most traditional campuses heatedly debate the extent to which they will enter this market and whether it will lead to a sweeping reinvention of how students and faculty teach, learn, and conduct scholarship or whether it merely is a technological resource to be used like any other. The current technology has at least five unique features: its rapid development and rate of change, the extent to which its applications are being adopted in all areas of modern life beyond the campus, its widespread availability nationally—even globally—in a short time span, its potential for use with few constraints of time and location, and its increased affordability as it gets more powerful. These features make it imperative that institutions adopt it as a tool, but their capacity to use technology for educational purposes is perhaps the most critical challenge that postsecondary institutions must face. The irony is that this technology, which was spawned in universities, has taken on a life of its own. With so many societal as well as educational applications and implications, it has created its own industry as new computer hardware and software, telecommunications, and information-handling products and firms are developed. The impacts on the postsecondary industry and its institutions will be extensive, and perhaps central, in the next decade (Gilbert and Green, 1995; Twigg, 1994).

On the one hand, this technological revolution has a vast potential for increasing the array of options for accessing electronic learning opportunities, for reaching a significant array of new customers (students or scholars), and for extending an institution's potential to serve. On the other hand, it has in many instances reversed the supplier-client relationship between postsecondary institutions and telematics firms. Instead of being the customer seeking an institution's research results or trained students, these firms have become both the creators and suppliers of information-handling tools, making the postsecondary institutions increasingly dependent on these former clients. An even bigger threat is the array of postsecondary and nonpostsecondary organizations that are both new entrants and substitute suppliers in the current postsecondary educational industry. A rapidly growing number of institutions and organizations offering postsecondary education via interactive telecommunications have emerged, and others are beginning to experiment with this mode (Marchese, 1998). Large companies are adopting these technologies for their own internal postsecondary training programs. Of greater significance are the possible mergers of entertainment and telecommunication firms, which further enhance the potential for delivering postsecondary knowledge. (Will they make education entertaining or entertainment more educational?) For current postsecondary institutions this revolution has the potential to alter significantly the core technology of teaching, learning, and research. The availability and control of information, the role of faculty, the role of the learner, the process of learning, and even the process of research may all be changed radically.

Clearly, what makes this change so revolutionary is that it also interacts with all the other societal challenges. Despite often high initial investment costs, colleges and universities cannot afford *not* to employ this technology. It enhances the capacity to reach both new and current customers, or students, differently. It also influences the way academics work and students learn. This technology is just beginning to reshape the way postsecondary institutions compete with each other for students and compete or cooperate with firms in other industries (such as telematics, entertainment, and training) to deliver their educational products. New patterns of competition and cooperation with firms that were not part of the postsecondary industry are emerging as they and colleges and universities become part of a postsecondary knowledge industry that delivers educational services. The major challenge is to develop new interinstitutional ties with telematics firms in appropriate educational ventures.

Academic and Institutional Quality Reform. The challenge to academic and institutional quality is the outcome of somewhat separate conditions. In the 1990s, the demand for educational quality has become pervasive (Ewell, 1997), but in the 1960s and 1970s, quality was associated with the level and nature of institutional resources. In the 1980s, the focus shifted to assessing results (outcomes, goal achievement, added value). In the mid-1990s, academic quality has become associated with public accountability and with a focus on student learning, faculty productivity and performance, program effectiveness, and even institutional performance indicators. The debate about the definition of, criteria for, and means of improving educational quality shows no signs of diminishing and will be a continuing challenge both in governmental policy circles and in institutional discussions (Dill and Sporn, 1995).

A more recent focus on institutional quality is the interest in Total Quality Management (TQM) or continuous quality improvement (CQI) (Marchese, 1997), which emerged in the private sector. Unlike the more educationally focused notions of quality, this approach suggests a more comprehensive emphasis on developing an institutional culture that stresses policies and practices promoting an environment of continuous improvement; customer or client centeredness; a rational approach to decision making, using intensive measurement and benchmarking; a focus on process design; collaboration and teamwork; and individual empowerment. Such a comprehensive approach clashes with colleges' and universities' strong traditions of academic individualism but may also lead to their rethinking teaching, learning, and research processes and how they use the new technology for educational purposes. The fact that the Baldridge Award was extended in 1995 to include postsecondary education suggests that the quality movement may have a continued emphasis in academic as well as administrative areas.

To date, the quality challenges of TQM and CQI have had limited but differing impacts on the postsecondary industry. However, that may increase as competition within the industry, public scrutiny, and cost pressures increase. Both force institutions to refocus on defining and differentiating their stakeholders (customers needs and demands) and on designing their services (academic or administrative) with stakeholders in mind. Although neither has yet prompted the entry of new organizations in postsecondary education, numerous assessment and evaluation groups are now providing services for postsecondary institutions. More important, many of the new technology-based institutions emphasize both assessment and quality principles. This challenge may shape public support and the competition for students.

Economic Productivity: New Emphasis or New Function? Economic development has always been a factor in the rapid and continual expansion of postsecondary education (Leslie and Brinkman, 1988). Colleges and universities produced well-trained students, provided appropriate professional programs, and conducted pure and applied research that contributed to society's well-being, which, they argued, led to improvement in our standard of living. But the decline of U.S. economic fortunes in the past two decades and the loss of dominance in key manufacturing industries in the global marketplace has led to a new emphasis on enhancing economic productivity at the national, state, and regional level.

In federal priorities and state-level plans for economic development, higher education institutions, governmental agencies, and private business organizations are all viewed as key players. Postsecondary institutions have historically played, and been satisfied with playing, a *knowledge development* function as primary providers of academic and professional training and of pure and applied research. In recent decades, as consultants and as sites for campus research parks, they have participated more directly in *technology transfer.* A more recent and aggressive form of this activity is reflected in the growth of campus-affiliated incubator parks for new product and new company development. Most recently, postsecondary institutions have participated in developing "state or regional economic development strategies." In all these roles, their participation can vary from resource institution to partner to manager of the function (Peterson, 1985). Increasingly, institutions are pressured to take on all three roles and even to become leaders of the effort. The difficulty is that becoming a manager of technology transfer or economic development may involve an institution in an activity for which it is not well suited and one in which it may not be able to succeed (Feller, 1990). Yet political and economic pressures to show greater institutional accountability and contribution in this area is likely to increase if our economy falters or fails to meet political expectations or promises.

This challenge has little direct affect on students as postsecondary institutions' primary customers, although some argue it is reflected in students' career-oriented priorities and concerns about useful programs. However, it does subject the industry to increasing demands from its primary government and industry suppliers, especially in the public sector. The growing concern for economic productivity also attracts public and private technology development organizations, both as new entrants and as substitute sources of this activity, that may be better positioned than postsecondary institutions to compete for applied research and development funds and better staffed to carry out such activities. Existing postsecondary institutions that decide to participate may need to subsidize risky economic development activities and to create an economic development alliance, a technology transfer partnership, or a joint venture to provide this new service. In doing so they may be pressed to redirect some funds and effort away from their traditional emphasis on teaching and research in order to supply the needs of the economic development activity. In most instances this pressure for economic development involves postsecondary education directly in a new realm of competition: interregional, interstate, or even international—an arena in which it was previously only indirectly engaged.

Postsecondary Relearning: New Markets, Modes, and Models. In recent decades, expanded educational services have been directed toward increasing traditional student enrollments and increasing service to underrepresented groups such as minorities, women, and older students. Modifications in schedules (extending classes to evenings and weekends) and locale (supplying instruction off campus) were used to deliver traditional courses or programs to the part-time, nontraditional student. Continuing education was often an ancillary function or one primarily related to professional and occupational programs. Yet in today's increasingly competitive and technologically turbulent world, products, companies, and careers can change rapidly. The need for technological retooling and postsecondary reeducation is increasing in a wide variety of professions (Reich, 1991).

The demand from older individuals for postsecondary relearning is an exploding market consisting of three identifiable groups. One is the post–high school but prebaccalaureate group, individuals who need further education to reenter the job market or remain viably employed. One study (Grubb, in press) suggests this category includes twenty to thirty million individuals between twenty-five and fifty years of age. A second is the post-baccalaureate group, individuals who have college degrees but may need further education although not necessarily degree education to remain viably employed or to change fields. Though not as large as the previous group, it is rapidly growing as the proportion of degree holders continues to grow. Finally, there are the graduate and professional degree holders, individuals who need more than the traditional continuing education in their professional fields to advance or change fields. In addition to size and growth, the members of these three market segments have much in common. Their educational interests, or those of their employers, often focus on professional competencies, individual educational needs, learning modules, off-campus delivery, and willingness to use distance education modes of transmission (including technology) rather than on traditional courses, degrees, or programs.

The existence of these three groups suggests substantial numbers of potential customers for postsecondary reeducation. Although some may pay for their own education, many employer organizations are clients for such educational services for their employees. Indeed some large companies and some industries are either supporting or developing their own providers. It is a market that many in the proprietary sector see as an economic opportunity as well as a large, underserved educational market, and it has begun to attract many competing organizations, either as new entrants or as substitute sources. Some are existing postsecondary institutions; some are new postsecondary institutions. Education and training firms and entertainment and telecommunication firms are involved, and there are various alliances. In some instances, political entities such as the Western Governors organization and individual states are promoting these developments. Virtual institutions of varied types are also emerging (Carchidi and Peterson, 1998; Marchese, 1998). Almost all emphasize new modes of packaging and delivery and emphasize learner-centered education. But this market is still somewhat amorphous. Patterns of market demand, financing, and competition are not well defined and neither is the role to be played by traditional postsecondary institutions.

Globalization: Breaking Bonds and Boundaries. As we enter the twenty-first century, the challenges of international and global perspectives need little exposition. International student and faculty exchange programs, an emphasis on foreign language instruction, and the introduction of global perspectives into curricula are widespread if not completely effective measures. But two emergent phenomena suggest the globalization in postsecondary education could take on new institutional boundary–spanning forms in the near future.

Although knowledge and scholars have always resisted regional and national boundaries, new international networks are emerging. These *international civil societies* (Cohen, 1997) are networks of university scholars, governmental policy researchers, and private sector experts organized around major significant social problems or issues (global warming, AIDS, human rights, and the like). These civil societies are interdisciplinary, cross-national, and cross-industry. Their work may combine research, learning, policymaking, and action. They often rely on technology and may have access to a wide array of information and expertise but have little managerial structure. In effect they reflect how the knowledge and technology explosion can rewrite scholarly boundaries independently of institutional structure.

Another form of globalization that may emerge is more similar to the multinational corporation. Loosely structured institutional exchange programs and research alliances that cross national boundaries are common, but now the prospects for a multinational university are worth contemplating. Some universities now have campuses in other countries. Many postsecondary institutions have partnerships with multinational technology firms. Some governmental entities, such as the European Union, have supported cross-national postsecondary alliances. Moves to more formal international consortia, to degree-granting federations among institutions in different countries, and even to a multinational university, though a daunting challenge, are possible in the decade ahead.

Clearly, scholars, researchers, and many students who already participate in less formal educational arrangements constitute a specialized customer group that could be attracted. Some countries, as clients, might support limited forms of cross-national alliances and embrace institutions with an extensive cross-national mission or presence. Currently, some postsecondary institutions do function multinationally to a limited degree, and some of the emerging institutions that focus on distance education via technology have identified this as their niche. But truly multinational postsecondary educational organizations would be an intriguing new entrant to the postsecondary industry and would provide a new global opportunity for study and scholarship. As some authors note, these new forms of global organization may markedly intensify competition in postsecondary education (Dill and Sporn, 1995).

The Emerging Postsecondary Knowledge Industry

As we enter the twenty-first century, the changing societal conditions I have discussed are all likely to continue. Each promises to have a major impact on the six forces that are reshaping the current postsecondary industry into a more comprehensive knowledge industry. Table 8.3 outlines a paradigm of this industry, showing the six forces at work in the left-hand column, the existing industry conditions in the middle column, and the emerging knowledge industry conditions in the right-hand column.

Innovation in Core Technology. Perhaps the most influential force is the potential for innovation in core technology—the development, transmission, and dissemination of knowledge in society and in turn in the

**Table 8.3. Paradigm of an Emerging Postsecondary
Knowledge Industry**

Six Industry Forces	Existing Industry	Emerging Knowledge Network
Innovation in core technology	Traditional teaching, learning, research modes	Interactive information technology (IT) network for teaching learning, research, and scholarship
Threat of new entrants	Traditional colleges, universities, and proprietary institutions	Telecommunications, computing hardware and software, information resource, corporate and governmental education and training, and entertainment firms
Power of customers (students)	Traditional and nontraditional degree students	Growing minority and postsecondary relearning markets for individual learning needs
Power of suppliers (clients)	Primarily employers, funding sources, and purchasers of services	Providers of information resources, educational technology, and communications networks—as pressure groups, partners, or competitors
Threat of substitute services	Limited	More extensive
Intensity of competition	Among existing postsecondary	Cross-industry—more competitive and entrepreneurial institutions or segments

postsecondary industry. Postsecondary institutions have long believed they were the preeminent knowledge industry for postsecondary teaching, learning, and research. However, the telematics revolution has introduced a powerful new interactive information-handling technology that offers potentially revolutionary changes, moving from more traditional modes of teaching, learning, and research to varied, responsive, flexible, interactive, and individualized modes. The technology revolution has allowed institutions from outside traditional postsecondary education to become leaders in reshaping both the basic technology and the industry of postsecondary education. More critically, the telematics revolution makes it easier for institutions to respond to all the other societal conditions affecting the industry (diversity, quality reform, economic productivity, postsecondary relearning, and globalization), and this revolution enhances all six of the forces acting upon the industry (not just the innovation in core technology but also the threat of new organizational entrants, the power of customers, the power of suppliers, the threat of substitute services, and the intensity of competition).

Threat of New Entrants. The threat of new organizational entrants is suggested by five of the six societal conditions (diversity, telematics, economic productivity, relearning, and globalization). Perhaps the most tangible way of visualizing the reconfiguration of the industry is to focus on the organizations that are becoming part of a postsecondary knowledge industry. Postsecondary education is now offered by a broad array of public, private, and proprietary educational organizations from associate degree to doctoral degree level. The emergence of a postsecondary knowledge industry suggests the addition of many organizations previously thought to be part of other industries: telecommunication companies; computer software and hardware firms; information resource organizations; corporate and governmental organizations engaged in education, training, and professional development; and perhaps even entertainment firms. As the previous discussion has suggested, these new organizations are often no longer either just suppliers to or customers of postsecondary institutions. They are now effectively part of the postsecondary knowledge development, dissemination, and education system and may be viewed as potential collaborators or competitors.

The Power of Customers. The analysis of all six societal conditions also suggests implications for potential student markets for postsecondary education. In addition to both traditional and nontraditional students seeking regular course credits and degree offerings via traditional delivery modes, there are potential new students, customers who are interested in non-degree-oriented learning and often in nontraditional modes of delivery. The key shift in the postsecondary knowledge industry perspective is to focus on students as learners with individual educational needs rather than to see them as users of courses and programs designed and delivered by postsecondary faculty or institutions. This shift is a process of moving from *just-in-case* to *just-in-time* to *just-for-you* education (Duderstadt, 1998).

Power of Suppliers and Threat of Substitute Services. The potential for new noneducational organization entrants to the emerging postsecondary knowledge industry is implied by each of the societal conditions. These conditions not only enhance their role as customers but also change their role as suppliers. As customers for particular types of postsecondary education for their employees, they are now more active and aggressive in defining and demanding educational needs and learning experiences. But they are no longer just customers who employ graduates, purchase knowledge products and services, or provide sources of funding. They are often also key suppliers of valuable information resources, new educational technology, and access to critical communication networks. Another major shift is that in the new postsecondary knowledge environment these noneducational participants may be sources of substitute educational services. Further, they are now potential pressure groups and educational partners or competitors. It is clear that in a postsecondary knowledge environment these knowledge-based firms have acquired greater power as suppliers of educational resources and as customers for or sources of substitute services because they control educational information technology and access to customers for learning.

Intensity of Competition. Finally, it is apparent that the level of competition in the postsecondary knowledge industry is likely to increase. Clearly, competition among existing postsecondary institutions is intensified by the challenges to increase diversity, to use technology, to improve quality, to contribute to economic productivity, to become more global, and to enter the expanding postsecondary relearning markets while also constraining costs. However, what is likely to be qualitatively different is competition that cuts across old industry boundaries. For instance, competing with organizations whose primary function is not education—organizations from the telecommunications, computing, information resource, corporate education and training, or entertainment industry worlds—is far more entrepreneurial and fast paced than is competing with other traditional postsecondary institutions. Also competition to engage in economic development or new global arrangements may entail both creative risk taking and new governmental controls or regulatory environments.

Clearly, no one knows yet the exact direction in which the postsecondary knowledge industry will emerge or its comprehensiveness, its rate of development, and its full impact on current postsecondary institutions. Neither do we know whether those changes will be evolutionary and manageable or revolutionary and chaotic. They will no doubt affect different types of institutions differently, and some will see them as opportunity and others as threat.

Implications: The New Management, Organization, and Performance Focus. Although the precise implications of this emerging industry may be unclear, the change is different in magnitude from previous industry transactions and too critical for institutional leaders and researchers not to address. Institutions must consider whether to take a proactive, adaptive, or responsive strategy toward the emerging industry and define their institutional role in it. They will need to consider the managerial challenge to redesign themselves. New organizational models reflecting institutional responses to this new industry are already emerging. They include entrepreneurial, network, and virtual organizations and also new forms of strategic alliances and joint ventures with noneducational partners for the design, dissemination, and discovery of knowledge. As postsecondary institutions address redesign, their long-term performance criteria will also change. These criteria may be assessed by how well each institution addresses and answer those four R's of the next decade. How well has it

Redefined the nature of a postsecondary knowledge industry and its role in that industry?

Redirected the institution's mission and developed new external relationships to reflect these new realities?

Reorganized or restructured academic processes and delivery systems? *Reformed* the academic workplace and institutional culture?

Institutional Research for Institutional Redesign

The implications for an institutional research office whose institutional leadership focuses on this emerging new industry and examines the need for institutional redesign include a new role or function and several related activities.

Postsecondary Knowledge Industry Analyst. In an emergent industry with rapidly changing participants and dynamics, institutional leadership will need to understand the new environment and its institutional implications. For the institutional researcher, becoming a postsecondary knowledge industry analyst will involve becoming the institution's expert on the various segments of the postsecondary relearning markets for both degree and nondegree, nontraditional, and older student consumers; on which postsecondary institutions and nonpostsecondary organizations are offering postsecondary learning experiences for those markets; on the varied strategies and methods for delivering postsecondary learning on and off campus; on the new forms of technology-based delivery, including virtual learning systems; and on the forms of strategic alliances, joint ventures, and other interinstitutional linkages developed to deliver postsecondary education, promote knowledge dissemination, and support research. Although this role may be analogous to an institutional researcher's role in environmental analysis for planning, it is focused more specifically on the emerging industry. The intent is not merely to inform institutional leaders but to assist them in developing new roles and strategies for the institution in this new industry, to become the institution's source of expertise on this new industry paradigm, its dynamics, and its implications for the institution. Implicit in this new function or role are several more specific activities.

Monitoring Social and Industry Conditions. This chapter has suggested several changing societal conditions that influence the emerging postsecondary knowledge industry and these conditions might be monitored by the IR office. Among the other areas that will affect the emerging industry and that also come to mind are the role states and accrediting agencies adopt in regulating the industry; changes in patterns of financial support for students, including older students and those pursuing non-degree-oriented education (financial aid, tax credits or vouchers, company employment benefits, and so forth); the cost structure of access to the Internet; the financial structure of technology-based providers (technology investment, course development costs, student fees and charges). Although monitoring social and industry conditions may be similar to environmental scanning, the key is to focus on conditions that have implications for the entire industry as well as for your institution. A major contribution will be to develop indicators for these conditions and for the emerging industry. A major complicating factor is knowing how to define the scope of such indicators when the advent of technology-based delivery systems is making markets, participating organizations, and delivery systems less geographically bounded.

Reviewing Strategic Options. As institutions redefine the role they intend to play in this emerging industry, reshape their external relationships, and reorganize their delivery systems, proposed new joint ventures, strategic alliances, and other interinstitutional arrangements with nonpostsecondary partners will emerge. These will need to be compared with existing or more institutionally controlled approaches. These new approaches may involve major new investments—not simple modifications or small pilot efforts. IR reviews of such strategic options might include carefully analyzing the market potential for the proposed venture (in markets that are still being created or are ill defined); examining the organizational, legal, and fiscal requirements of joint efforts and the managerial capacity needed to run them; conducting studies of the impact of new ventures on the current institution; and doing a careful resource investment and risk analysis. These are no longer simple program reviews of new academic programs with marginal resource reallocations.

Monitoring the Periphery. Robert Zemsky (1997) has pointed out that in many postsecondary institutions the changes that respond to the new postsecondary knowledge industry demands are on the periphery of the institution. Most institutions continue to manage their traditional core degree programs and research activities and give little attention to the new ventures until they become dominant or the source of mismanagement or embarrassment. Monitoring an institution's peripheral activities as a good management servant will include keeping track of things such as the extended delivery academic programs and the joint ventures or alliances in research, education, and service; the growing enrollment and employment patterns for these activities; and the revenue and expense patterns. These activities may also need to undergo a fiscal vulnerability audit related to these activities. More basically IR staff need to understand and be able to communicate the balance between an institution's core and periphery efforts and its shifting priorities in relation to its mission, role, and managerial capacity.

Assessing and Reviewing Programs. Many of the new educational, research, and service ventures that respond to this new industry will require new performance criteria, new management approaches, and new external partners. Programs delivered by technology or based on a specialized or individualized design are especially problematic. Extending assessment and program review to such new ventures and perhaps conducting these activities with new external and noneducational partners is critical to assuring quality of the efforts. It will be challenging to undertake and will require new approaches.

Changing Institutional Assessment. An institution undergoing extensive change or transformation, particularly if it is an intentional redesign, needs to mount efforts to assess its academic and administrative capacity to undertake the planned changes; to understand the tensions between traditional or core programs and newer, more peripheral ones; and to understand the changing external image resulting from intentional institutional mission and role changes. Assessing both the readiness and capacity for institutional change will become central to successful redesign.

Proactive Management Guide. In sum, this last discussion provides institutional researchers with a substantial new role and set of activities. Clearly, the extent of this role of postsecondary industry knowledge analyst will vary by institution type, size, and current mission; by the way in which planning and institutional research are organized; and by key institutional leaders' willingness to address the challenge of an emergent postsecondary knowledge industry and the possibility of institutional redesign. Again, whether the actual shift will be evolutionary or revolutionary is unclear. But institutional research once again has the opportunity of assisting in and shaping major institutional response to a major challenge and of going beyond its traditional management service and institutional improvement function. By becoming a proactive management guide to this new industry and environment, institutional research will once again have played its adaptive function—benefiting both the institution and the profession.

MARVIN W. PETERSON is professor of higher education at the Center for the Study of Higher and Postsecondary Education at the University of Michigan, and research program director for the National Center for Postsecondary Improvement.

References

AIR Forum Evaluation Committee. "Evaluation of the 1994 Association for Institutional Research Forum, New Orleans, LA." Report to the AIR Board of Directors, June 1994.

AIR Forum Evaluation Committee. "1998 Association for Institutional Research Forum, Minneapolis, MN: Luncheon Survey Results." Report to the AIR Board of Directors, May 1998.

Allen, R., and Chaffee, E. E. "Management Fads in Higher Education." Unpublished paper, National Center for Higher Education Management Systems, Boulder, Colo., 1981.

Alpert, D. "Performance and Paralysis: The Organizational Context of the American Research University." *Journal of Education,* 1986, *56* (3).

Argyris, C., and Schön, D. A. *Theory in Practice: Increasing Professional Effectiveness.* San Francisco: Jossey-Bass, 1974.

Argyris, C., and Schön, D. A. *Organizational Learning: A Theory of Action Perspective.* Reading, Mass.: Addison-Wesley, 1978.

Balderston, F. E., and Weathersby, G. B. *PPBS in Higher Education Planning and Management: From PPBS to Policy Analysis.* Report P-31. Berkeley: Ford Foundation Program for Research in University Administration, University of California, May 1972.

Baldridge, J. V. *Power and Conflict in the University.* New York: Wiley, 1971.

Bartlett, F. C. *Remembering: A Study in Experimental and Social Psychology.* Cambridge, England: Cambridge University Press, 1932.

Berdahl, R. O. *Statewide Coordination of Higher Education.* Washington, D.C.: American Council on Education, 1971.

Billups, F. D., and DeLucia, L. A. "Integrating Institutional Research into the Organization." In J. B. Presley (ed.), *Organizing Effective Institutional Research Offices.* New Directions for Institutional Research, no. 66. San Francisco: Jossey-Bass, 1990.

Birnbaum, R. *How Colleges Work: The Cybernetics of Academic Organization and Leadership.* San Francisco: Jossey-Bass, 1988.

Blau, P. M. *Exchange and Power in Social Life.* New York: Wiley, 1964.

Bowen, H. R. (ed.). *Evaluating Institutions for Accountability.* New Directions for Institutional Research, no. 1. San Francisco: Jossey-Bass, 1974.

Brubacher, J., and Rudy, W. *Higher Education in Transition: A History of American Colleges and Universities, 1636–1968.* (Rev. ed.) New York: HarperCollins, 1968.

Brumbaugh, A. J. *Research Designed to Improve Institutions of Higher Learning.* Washington, D.C.: American Council on Education, 1960.

Bruner, J. S. *The Process of Education.* (2nd ed.) Cambridge, Mass.: Harvard University Press, 1963.

Carchidi, D. M., and Peterson, M. W. *The Emerging Organizational Landscape of Postsecondary Education.* Ann Arbor: Center for the Study of Higher and Postsecondary Education, University of Michigan, 1998.

Carnegie Foundation for the Advancement of Teaching. *The Control of the Campus: A Report on the Governance of Higher Education.* Princeton, N.J.: Princeton University Press, 1982.

Carter, D. J., and Wilson, R. *Minorities in Higher Education: 1992 Eleventh Annual Status Report.* Washington, D.C.: American Council on Education, 1993.

Cartter, A. *An Assessment of Quality in Graduate Education.* Washington, D.C.: American Council on Education, 1966.

Clark, B. R. "Belief and Loyalty in College Organization." *Journal of Higher Education,* 1971, *42* (6).

Cleveland, H. *The Knowledge Executive: Leadership in an Information Society.* New York: Truman Talley Books, 1985.

Cohen, D. W. "Understanding the Globalization of Scholarship." In M. W. Peterson, D. D. Dill, and L. A. Mets (eds.), *Planning and Management for a Changing Environment.* San Francisco: Jossey-Bass, 1997.

Cohen, M. D., and March, J. G. *Leadership and Ambiguity: The American College President.* New York: McGraw-Hill, 1974.

Cohen, M. D., March, J. G., and Olsen, J. P. "A Garbage Can Model of Organizational Choice." *Administrative Science Quarterly,* 1972, *17* (1), 1–25.

Commission on Colleges of the Southern Association of Colleges and Schools. *Criteria for Accreditation.* (9th ed.) Decatur, Ga.: Commission on Colleges of the Southern Association of Colleges and Schools, 1995.

Commission on Higher Education. *Framework for Outcomes Assessment.* Philadelphia: Middle States Association of Colleges and Schools, 1996.

Cope, R. G. (ed.). *Professional Development for Institutional Research.* New Directions for Institutional Research, no. 23. San Francisco: Jossey-Bass, 1979.

de Geus, A. P. "Planning as Learning." *Harvard Business Review,* 1988, *88* (2), 70–74.

Delaney, A. M. "The Role of Institutional Research in Higher Education: Enabling Researchers to Meet New Challenges." *Research in Higher Education,* 1997, *38,* 116.

Dill, D. D., and Sporn, B. "University 2001: What Will the University of the Twenty-First Century Look Like?" In D. D. Dill and B. Sporn (eds.), *Emerging Patterns of Social Demand and University Reform: Through a Glass Darkly.* New York: Pergamon Press, 1995.

Dressel, P. L. "Nature of Institutional Research in Self-Study." In P. L. Dressel and Associates, *Institutional Research in the University: A Handbook.* San Francisco: Jossey-Bass, 1971.

Dressel, P. L. "The Shaping of Institutional Research and Planning." *Research in Higher Education,* 1981, *14* (3), 229–258.

Dressel, P. L., and Associates. *Institutional Research in the University.* San Francisco: Jossey-Bass, 1971.

Drucker, P. Interview. *Forbes Magazine,* 1995.

Duderstadt, J. J. "The Twenty-First Century University: A Tale of Two Futures." Paper presented at the North American and Western European Colloquium on the Challenges Facing Higher Education, Glion, Switzerland, May 13–17, 1998.

Dyer, H. S. "Can Institutional Research Lead to a Science of Institutions?" *Educational Record,* 1966, *47,* 452–466.

Endo, J. J. "Needs Assessment Survey Results Are Reported." *AIR Newsletter,* Winter 1989, pp. 6–7.

Endo, J. J., Dunn, J. A., Armijo, F., Melchiori, G. S., Pratt, L. K., Skubal, J. M., and Van Middlesworth, C. L. "An Assessment of the Professional Development Needs of the Members of the Association for Institutional Research." Report by the Professional Development Services Board to the AIR Executive Board, Sept. 1988.

Ewell, P. T. *Refashioning Accountability: Toward a "Coordinated" System of Quality Assurance for Higher Education.* Denver, Colo.: Education Commission of the States, 1997.

Feller, I. "Universities as Engines of R&D-Based Economic Growth." *Research Policy,* 1990, *19* (4).

Fincher, C. "Policy Research and Analysis: The Choice of Models for Institutional Research." Paper presented at the Annual Forum of the Association for Institutional Research, Montreal, May 1977.

Fincher, C. "Institutional Research as Organizational Intelligence." *Research in Higher Education,* 1978, *8* (2), 189–192.

Fincher, C. "The Art and Science of Institutional Research." In M. W. Peterson and M. Corcoran (eds.), *Institutional Research in Transition.* New Directions for Institutional Research, no. 46. San Francisco: Jossey-Bass, 1985.

Firnberg, J. W., and Lasher, W. F. "The Future of Institutional Research." In J. W. Firnberg and W. F. Lasher (eds.), *The Politics and Pragmatics of Institutional Research.* New Directions for Institutional Research, no. 38. San Francisco: Jossey-Bass, 1983.

Friedland, E. I. *Introduction to the Concept of Rationality in Political Science.* Morristown, N.J.: General Learning Press, 1974.

Gaither, G., Nedwek, B. P., and Neal, J. E. *Measuring Up: The Promise and Pitfalls of Performance Indicators in Higher Education.* ASHE-ERIC Higher Education Report no. 5. Washington, D.C.: George Washington University, Graduate School of Education and Human Development, 1994.

Georgiou, P. "The Goal Paradigm and Notes Toward a Counter Paradigm." *Administrative Science Quarterly,* 1973, *18* (3), 291–331.

Gilbert, S. W., and Green, K. C. *Information Technology: A Road to the Future?* To Promote Academic Justice and Excellence Series. Washington, D.C.: Office of Higher Education, National Education Association, 1995.

Gill, J. I., and Saunders, L. (eds.). *Developing Effective Policy Analysis in Higher Education.* New Directions for Institutional Research, no. 76. San Francisco: Jossey-Bass, 1992.

Gioia, D. A. "Symbols, Scripts, and Sensemaking: Creating Meaning in the Organizational Experience." In H. P. Sims, Jr., and D. A. Gioia (eds.), *The Thinking Organization: Dynamics of Organizational Social Cognition.* San Francisco: Jossey-Bass, 1986.

Goodman, P. *Community of Scholars.* New York: Random House, 1964.

Graesser, A. C., Woll, S. B., Kowalski, D. J., and Smith, D. A. "Memory for Typical and Atypical Actions in Scripted Activities." *Journal of Experimental Psychology: Human Learning and Memory,* 1980, *6,* 503–515.

Gross, E. "The Definition of Organizational Goals." *British Journal of Sociology,* 1969, *20,* 277–294.

Harrington, C. F. "Assessing Institutional Research: A Practical Guide to Assessment Strategy." Paper presented at the AIR Forum, Boston, May 1995.

Harrington, C. F., and Chen, H. "The Characteristics, Roles and Functions of Institutional Research Professionals in the Southern Association for Institutional Research." Paper presented at the AIR Forum, Boston, May 1995. (ED 386 136)

Harrington, C. F., Knight, W., and Christie, R. "An Examination of Institutional Research Functions and Structures in Georgia Higher Education." Paper presented at the AIR Forum, New Orleans, May 1994. (ED 372 722)

Hearn, J. C., and Corcoran, M. E. "An Exploration of Factors Behind the Proliferation of the Institutional Research Enterprise." *Journal of Higher Education,* 1988, *59,* 634–651.

Hellman, C. "The State of Institutional Research in Oklahoma." Paper presented at the Oklahoma Association for Institutional Research conference, Oklahoma City, Oct. 1998.

Homans, G. *Social Behavior: Its Elementary Forms.* Orlando: Harcourt Brace, 1961.

Hunt, P. "Fallacy of the One Big Brain." *Harvard Business Review,* 1966, *44,* 84–90.

Huntington, R. B., and Clagett, C. A. "Increasing Institutional Research Effectiveness and Productivity: Findings from a National Survey." Research paper presented at the eighteenth annual conference of the North East Association for Institutional Research, Cambridge, Mass., Nov. 1991.

Ilchman, W. F., and Uphoff, N. T. *The Political Economy of Change.* Berkeley: University of California Press, 1969.

Jedamus, P., Peterson, M. W., and Associates. *Improving Academic Management: A Handbook of Planning and Institutional Research.* San Francisco: Jossey-Bass, 1980.

Johnson, F. C., and Christal, M. E. "Preparing for Self-Study." *The AIR Professional File,* 1985, *22,* 1–12.

Katz, D., and Kahn, R. *The Social Psychology of Organizations.* New York: Wiley, 1978.

Keller, G. *Academic Strategy: The Management Revolution in American Higher Education.* Baltimore: Johns Hopkins University Press, 1983.

Kerr, C. *The Uses of the University.* New York: HarperCollins, 1963.

Knight, W. E., Moore, M. E., and Coperthwaite, C. A. "Institutional Research: Knowledge, Skills, and Perceptions of Effectiveness. *Research in Higher Education,* 1997, *38,* 419–433.

Kotler, P. *Marketing for Non-Profit Organizations.* Englewood Cliffs, N.J.: Prentice Hall, 1975.

Kuhn, T. S. *The Structure of Scientific Revolutions.* (2nd ed.) Chicago: University of Chicago Press, 1970.

Lawrence, G. B., and Service, A. L. (eds.). *Quantitative Approaches to Higher Education Management: Potential, Limits, and Challenge.* AAHE-ERIC Research Report no. 4. Washington, D.C.: American Association of Higher Education, 1977.

Leslie, L. L., and Brinkman, P. T. *The Economic Value of Higher Education.* San Francisco: Jossey-Bass, 1988.

Lindblom, C. E. "The Science of Muddling Through." *Public Administration Review,* 1959, *19* (2), 79–88.

Lindquist, J. (ed.). *Increasing the Use of Program Evaluation.* New Directions for Institutional Research, no. 32. San Francisco: Jossey-Bass, 1981.

Lindquist, S. B. "AIR Membership Profile from AIR Membership Survey: Fall 1994." *The Electronic AIR* (on-line journal), July 11, 1995a, *15* (9). [www.fsu.edu/~air/eair.htm].

Lindquist, S. B. "Summary of the Findings of the 1994–95 AIR Membership Survey." Report to the AIR Board of Directors, Mar. 1995b.

Lord, R. G., and Foti, R. J. "Schema Theories, Information Processing, and Organizational Behavior." In H. P. Sims, Jr., and D. A. Gioia (eds.), *The Thinking Organization: Dynamics of Organizational Social Cognition.* San Francisco: Jossey-Bass, 1986.

Marchese, T. M. "Sustaining Quality Enhancement in Academic and Managerial Life." M. W. Peterson, D. D. Dill, and L. A. Mets (eds.), *Planning and Management for a Changing Environment.* San Francisco: Jossey-Bass, 1997.

Marchese, T. M. "Not-So-Distant Competitors." *AAHE Bulletin,* 1998, *50* (9).

McKinney, E. B., and Hindera, J. J. "Science and Institutional Research: The Links." Paper presented at the Annual Forum of the Association for Institutional Research, San Francisco, May 1991.

Millett, J. D. *The Academic Community.* New York: McGraw-Hill, 1962.

Mortimer, K. P. *Accountability in Higher Education.* ASHE/ERIC Report no. 1. Washington, D.C.: American Association for Higher Education, 1972.

Mortimer, K. P., and Tierney, M. L. *The Three R's of the Eighties: Reduction, Reallocation, and Retrenchment.* ASHE-ERIC Research Report no. 4. Washington, D.C.: American Association for Higher Education, 1979.

Muffo, J. A., and McLaughlin, G. W. (eds.). *A Primer on Institutional Research.* Tallahassee, Fla.: Association for Institutional Research, 1987.

Musil, C. M., and others. *Diversity in Higher Education: A Work in Progress.* Washington, D.C.: Association of American Colleges and Universities, 1995.

National Commission on Excellence in Education. *A Nation at Risk.* Washington, D.C.: U.S. Department of Education, 1983.

Noble, J. P. *1998 AIR Membership Survey Highlights.* Report to the AIR Board of Directors, Mar. 1999.

Pascarella, E. T., and Terenzini, P. T. *How College Affects Students: Findings and Insights from Twenty Years of Research.* San Francisco: Jossey-Bass, 1991.

Peters, R. "Accountability and the End(s) of Higher Education." *Change,* Nov.–Dec. 1994, pp. 16–23.

Peterson, M. W. "Analyzing Alternative Approaches to Planning." In P. Jedamus, M. W. Peterson, and Associates, *Improving Academic Management: A Handbook of Planning and Institutional Research.* San Francisco: Jossey Bass, 1980.

Peterson, M. W. "Institutional Research: An Evolutionary Perspective." In M. W. Peterson and M. Corcoran (eds.), *Institutional Research in Transition.* New Directions for Institutional Research, no. 46. San Francisco: Jossey-Bass, 1985.

Peterson, M. W., and Corcoran, M. (eds.). *Institutional Research in Transition.* New Directions for Institutional Research, no. 46. San Francisco: Jossey-Bass, 1985.

Peterson, M. W., Dill, D. D., and Mets, L. A. *Planning and Management for a Changing Environment.* San Francisco: Jossey-Bass, 1997.

Porter, M. *Competitive Strategy.* New York: Free Press, 1980.

Presley, J. B. "Putting the Building Blocks into Place for Effective Institutional Research." In J. B. Presley (ed.), *Organizing Effective Institutional Research Offices.* New Directions for Institutional Research, no. 66. San Francisco: Jossey-Bass, 1990.

Rapoport, A. "The Search for Simplicity." In E. Laszlo (ed.), *The Relevance of General Systems Theory: Papers Presented to Ludwig von Bertalantfy on His Seventieth Birthday.* New York: Braziller, 1972.

Reich, R. *The Work of Nations: Preparing Ourselves for Twenty-First Century Capitalism.* New York: Knopf, 1991.

Reichard, D. J. "Preliminary Results of Needs Assessment Survey Reported." *AIR Newsletter,* Fall 1981, p. 6.

Reichard, D. J. "Areas of Institutional Research Activity Cited in Responses to Professional Development Needs Assessment Survey." *AIR Newsletter,* Summer 1982a, p. 3.

Reichard, D. J. "Personal and Institutional Characteristics Reported." *AIR Newsletter,* Winter–Spring 1982b, p. 6.

Roose, K. D., and Anderson, C. J. *A Rating of Graduate Programs.* Washington, D.C.: American Council on Education, 1970.

Rourke, F. E., and Brooks, G. E. *The Managerial Revolution in Higher Education.* Baltimore: Johns Hopkins University Press, 1966.

Rudolph, F. *The American College and University.* New York: Vintage Books, 1962.

Sanford, N. (ed.) *The American College: A Psychological and Social Interpretation of Higher Learning.* New York: Wiley, 1962.

Saupe, J. L. *The Functions of Institutional Research.* Tallahassee, Fla.: Association for Institutional Research, 1981.

Saupe, J. L. *The Functions of Institutional Research.* (2nd ed.) Tallahassee, Fla.: Association for Institutional Research, 1990.

Schiltz, M. E. "An Introduction to the Draft Code of Ethics." In M. E. Schiltz (ed.), *Ethics and Standards in Institutional Research.* New Directions for Institutional Research, no. 73. San Francisco: Jossey-Bass, 1992.

Schmidtlein, F. A. "Information Systems and Concepts of Higher Education Governance." In C. R. Adams (ed.), *Appraising Information Needs of Decision Makers.* New Directions for Institutional Research, no. 15. San Francisco: Jossey-Bass, 1977.

Schmidtlein, F. A. "Comprehensive and Incremental Decision Paradigms and Their Implications for Educational Planning." In G. H. Copa and J. Moss, Jr. (eds.), *Planning and Vocational Education.* New York: McGraw-Hill, 1983.

Selznick, P. *Leadership in Administration.* New York: HarperCollins, 1957.

Shale, D., and Gomes, J. "A Longitudinal and Comparative View of the Organization and Functions of Offices of Institutional Research and Planning." Paper presented at the AIR Forum, Louisville, Ky., May 15, 1990.

Sharp, B. H. (ed.). *Association for Institutional Research Factbook.* (4th ed.) Tallahassee, Fla.: Association for Institutional Research, 1989.

Sheehan, B. S. "Developing Effective Information Systems." In P. Jedamus, M. W. Peterson, and Associates, *Improving Academic Management: A Handbook of Planning and Institutional Research.* San Francisco: Jossey-Bass, 1980.

Sheehan, B. S. (ed.). *Information Technology: Advances and Applications.* New Directions for Institutional Research, no. 35. San Francisco: Jossey-Bass, 1982.

Stroup, H. *Bureaucracy in Higher Education.* New York: Free Press, 1966.

Study Group on the Condition of Excellence in American Higher Education. *Involvement in Learning.* Washington, D.C.: National Institute of Education, 1984.

Taylor, S. E., and Crocker, J. "Schematic Biases of Social Information Processing." In E. T. Higgins, C. P. Herman, and M. P. Zanna (eds.), *Social Cognition: The Ontario Symposium.* Vol. 1. Hillsdale, N.J.: Erlbaum, 1981.

Terenzini, P. T. "On the Nature of Institutional Research and the Knowledge and Skills It Requires." *Research in Higher Education,* 1993, *34,* 1–10.

Tetlow, W. L. (ed.). *Using Microcomputers for Planning and Management Support.* New Directions for Institutional Research, no. 44. San Francisco: Jossey-Bass, 1984.

Tierney, W. G. (ed.). *Assessing Academic Climates and Cultures.* New Directions for Institutional Research, no. 68. San Francisco: Jossey-Bass, 1990.

Twigg, C. A. "The Changing Definition of Learning." *EDUCOM Review,* 1994, *29* (4), 23–25.

Vickers, G. *The Art of Judgment*. New York: Basic Books, 1965.

Volkwein, J. F. "State Regulation and Campus Autonomy." In J. C. Smart (ed.), *Higher Education: Handbook of Theory and Research*, Vol. 3. New York: Agathon Press, 1987.

Volkwein, J. F. "The Diversity of Institutional Research Structures and Tasks." In J. B. Presley (ed.), *Organizing Effective Institutional Research Offices*. New Directions for Institutional Research, no. 66. San Francisco: Jossey-Bass, 1990.

Volkwein, J. F. *Outcomes Assessment at Albany: A Summary of What We Have Learned Since 1978*. Institutional Research Report no. 12. Albany: Office of Institutional Research, State University of New York at Albany, 1992.

Volkwein, J. F. *The Undergraduate Experiences Most Strongly Associated with Ten Educational Outcomes at Albany*. Institutional Research Report no. 14. Albany: Office of Institutional Research, State University of New York at Albany, 1993.

Volkwein, J. F. *Promoting Student Success and Retention: A Summary of What Works*. Institutional Research Report no. 18. Albany: Office of Institutional Research, State University of New York at Albany, 1995.

Weick, K. E. *The Social Psychology of Organizing*. (2nd ed.) New York: Random House, 1979.

Whiteley, M. A., Porter, J. D., and Fenske, R. H. (eds.). *The Primer on Institutional Research*. Tallahassee, Fla.: Association for Institutional Research, 1992.

Wildavsky, A. *The Politics of the Budgetary Process*. Boston: Little, Brown, 1964.

Wildavsky, A. "The Political Economy of Efficiency: Cost-Benefit Analysis, Systems Analysis, and Program Budgeting." *Public Administration Review*, 1966, 26(4), 292–310.

Wilensky, H. L. *Organizational Intelligence: Knowledge and Policy in Government and Industry*. New York: Basic Books, 1969.

Wingspread Group on Higher Education. *An American Imperative: Higher Expectations for Higher Education*. Racine, Wisc.: Johnson Foundation, 1993

Yates, D. *Bureaucratic Democracy: The Search for Democracy and Efficiency in American Government*. Cambridge, Mass.: Harvard University Press, 1982.

Zemsky, R. AIR Forum address presented at the AIR Forum, Albuquerque, N. Mex., 1996.

INDEX

Back Issue/Subscription Order Form

Copy or detach and send to:
Jossey-Bass Inc., Publishers, 350 Sansome Street, San Francisco CA 94104-1342

Call or fax toll free!
Phone 888-378-2537 6AM-5PM PST; Fax 800-605-2665

Back issues   Please send me the following issues at $23 each:
(Important: please include series initials and issue number, such as IR90)

1. IR _____

_____

_____

$ _____ Total for single issues

$ _____ Shipping charges (for single issues **only;** subscriptions are exempt
from shipping charges): Up to $30, add $5^{50} • $30^{01}–$50, add $6^{50}
$50^{01}–$75, add $7^{50} • $75^{01}–$100, add $9 • $100^{01}–$150, add $10
Over $150, call for shipping charge

Subscriptions   Please ❏ start   ❏ renew my subscription to *New Directions
for Institutional Research* for the year ____ at the following rate:

❏ Individual $56   ❏ Institutional $99
NOTE: Subscriptions are quarterly and are for the calendar year only.
Subscriptions begin with the spring issue of the year indicated above.
For shipping outside the U.S., please add $25.

$ _____ Total single issues and subscriptions (CA, IN, NJ, NY, and DC
residents, add sales tax for single issues. NY and DC residents must
include shipping charges when calculating sales tax. NY and Canadian
residents only, add sales tax for subscriptions.)

❏ Payment enclosed (U.S. check or money order only)

❏ VISA, MC, AmEx, Discover Card #_____ Exp. date_____

Signature _____ Day phone _____

❏ Bill me (U.S. institutional orders only. Purchase order required.)

Purchase order #_____

Name _____

Address _____

_____

_____

Phone_____ E-mail _____

For more information about Jossey-Bass Publishers, visit our Web site at:
www.josseybass.com   **PRIORITY CODE = ND1**

United States Postal Service
Statement of Ownership, Management, and Circulation

1. Publication Title	2. Publication Number							3. Filing Date
NEW DIRECTIONS FOR INSTITUTIONAL RESEARCH	0 27	1	-	0	5	7	9	10/1/99

4. Issue Frequency	5. Number of Issues Published Annually	6. Annual Subscription Price
QUARTERLY	4	$ 56 - indiv. $ 99 - inst.

7. Complete Mailing Address of Known Office of Publication *(Not printer) (Street, city, county, state, and ZIP+4)*	Contact Person
350 SANSOME STREET SAN FRANCISCO, CA 94104 (SAN FRANCISCO COUNTY)	ROGER HUNT Telephone (415) 782-3232

8. Complete Mailing Address of Headquarters or General Business Office of Publisher *(Not printer)*

SAME AS ABOVE

9. Full Names and Complete Mailing Addresses of Publisher, Editor, and Managing Editor *(Do not leave blank)*

Publisher *(Name and complete mailing address)*

JOSSEY-BASS INC., PUBLISHERS
(ABOVE ADDRESS)

Editor *(Name and complete mailing address)*   J. FREDERICKS VOLKWEIN
PENNSYLVANIA STATE UNIVERSITY
403 SOUTH ALLEN STREET, SUITE 104
UNIVERSITY PARK, PA   16801-5252

Managing Editor *(Name and complete mailing address)*

NONE

10. Owner *(Do not leave blank. If the publication is owned by a corporation, give the name and address of the corporation immediately followed by the names and addresses of all stockholders owning or holding 1 percent or more of the total amount of stock. If not owned by a corporation, give the names and addresses of the individual owners. If owned by a partnership or other unincorporated firm, give its name and address as well as those of each individual owner. If the publication is published by a nonprofit organization, give its name and address.)*

Full Name	Complete Mailing Address
JOHN WILEY & SONS INC	605 THIRD AVENUE
	NEW YORK, NY 10158-0012

11. Known Bondholders, Mortgagees, and Other Security Holders Owning or Holding 1 Percent or More of Total Amount of Bonds, Mortgages, or Other Securities. If none, check box ⟶ ☐ None

Full Name	Complete Mailing Address
SAME AS ABOVE	SAME AS ABOVE
·	

12. Tax Status *(For completion by nonprofit organizations authorized to mail at nonprofit rates) (Check one)*
   The purpose, function, and nonprofit status of this organization and the exempt status for federal income tax purposes:
   ☐ Has Not Changed During Preceding 12 Months
   ☐ Has Changed During Preceding 12 Months *(Publisher must submit explanation of change with this statement)*

PS Form **3526**, September 1998   *(See Instructions on Reverse)*

13. Publication Title	14. Issue Date for Circulation Data Below
NEW DIRECTIONS FOR INSTITUTIONAL RESEARCH	SUMMER 1999

15. Extent and Nature of Circulation			Average No. Copies Each Issue During Preceding 12 Months	No. Copies of Single Issue Published Nearest to Filing Date
a. Total Number of Copies *(Net press run)*			1818	3745
b. Paid and/or Requested Circulation	(1)	Paid/Requested Outside-County Mail Subscriptions Stated on Form 3541. *(Include advertiser's proof and exchange copies)*	784	624
	(2)	Paid In-County Subscriptions *(Include advertiser's proof and exchange copies)*	0	0
	(3)	Sales Through Dealers and Carriers, Street Vendors, Counter Sales, and Other Non-USPS Paid Distribution	0	2500
	(4)	Other Classes Mailed Through the USPS	0	0
c. Total Paid and/or Requested Circulation *[Sum of 15b. (1), (2),(3),and (4)]*			784	3124
d. Free Distribution by Mail *(Samples, complimentary, and other free)*	(1)	Outside-County as Stated on Form 3541		
	(2)	In-County as Stated on Form 3541		
	(3)	Other Classes Mailed Through the USPS	0	0
e. Free Distribution Outside the Mail *(Carriers or other means)*			104	97
f. Total Free Distribution *(Sum of 15d. and 15e.)*			104	97
g. Total Distribution *(Sum of 15c. and 15f)*			888	3221
h. Copies not Distributed			930	524
i. Total *(Sum of 15g. and h.)*			1818	3745
j. Percent Paid and/or Requested Circulation *(15c. divided by 15g. times 100)*			88%	97%

16. Publication of Statement of Ownership

☒ Publication required. Will be printed in the ___WINTER 1999___ issue of this publication.   ☐ Publication not required.

17. Signature and Title of Editor, Publisher, Business Manager, or Owner SUSAN E. LEWIS
PERIODICALS DIRECTOR

Date 10/1/99

Signature: Susan E. Lewis

I certify that all information furnished on this form is true and complete. I understand that anyone who furnishes false or misleading information on this form or who omits material or information requested on the form may be subject to criminal sanctions (including fines and imprisonment) and/or civil sanctions (including civil penalties).

Instructions to Publishers

1. Complete and file one copy of this form with your postmaster annually on or before October 1. Keep a copy of the completed form for your records.

2. In cases where the stockholder or security holder is a trustee, include in items 10 and 11 the name of the person or corporation for whom the trustee is acting. Also include the names and addresses of individuals who are stockholders who own or hold 1 percent or more of the total amount of bonds, mortgages, or other securities of the publishing corporation. In item 11, if none, check the box. Use blank sheets if more space is required.

3. Be sure to furnish all circulation information called for in item 15. Free circulation must be shown in items 15d, e, and f.

4. Item 15h., Copies not Distributed, must include (1) newsstand copies originally stated on Form 3541, and returned to the publisher, (2) estimated returns from news agents, and (3), copies for office use, leftovers, spoiled, and all other copies not distributed.

5. If the publication had Periodicals authorization as a general or requester publication, this Statement of Ownership, Management, and Circulation must be published; it must be printed in any issue in October or, if the publication is not published during October, the first issue printed after October.

6. In item 16, indicate the date of the issue in which this Statement of Ownership will be published.

7. Item 17 must be signed.

Failure to file or publish a statement of ownership may lead to suspension of Periodocals authorization.

PS Form **3526,** September 1998 *(Reverse)*